CRAFTING THE RESISTANCE

35 PROJECTS FOR CRAFTIVISTS, PROTESTORS, AND WOMEN WHO PERSIST

LARA NEEL *and* HEATHER MARANO

Skyhorse Publishing

A portion of proceeds will be donated to Planned Parenthood.

Skyhorse Publishing books may be purchased in bulk at special discounts for sales promotion, corporate gifts, fund-raising, or educational purposes. Special editions can also be created to specifications. For details, contact the Special Sales Department, Skyhorse Publishing, 307 West 36th Street, 11th Floor, New York, NY 10018 or info@skyhorsepublishing.com.

Visit our website at www.skyhorsepublishing.com.

10 9 8 7 6 5 4 3 2 1

Library of Congress Cataloging-in-Publication Data is available on file.

Cover design by Jane Sheppard
Cover photo credit by Lara Neel and Heather Marano

Print ISBN: 978-1-5107-3138-7
Ebook ISBN: 978-1-5107-3139-4

Printed in the United States of America

DEDICATIONS

To my mama, who gave me my firm handshake, confident laugh, and strong voice. Also to my wife, who helps me sort out when to act and when to plan.
Lara

To my husband, for his unending support. And for my children, without whom life would just not be as beautiful.
Heather

TABLE OF CONTENTS

INTRODUCTIONS 1
A VERY SHORT HISTORY OF CRAFTIVISM 4
TIPS AND TRICKS 5
SPECIAL TOOLS 6

ON THE MARCH 13
Clarity Vinyl Tote 15
Go Anywhere, Say Anything Messenger Bag 21
Five Unbranded Bandannas 33
Purl-Free Pussyhats 45
Sewing a Flock of Fleece Pussyhats 51
Persistent Marker Message T-shirts 55
Security Waist Belt 59
Mobility Ankle Pocket 63
Bleeding Heart T-Shirt 67
Snowflake Wristers 73
Black Lives Matter Hat 77

AT HOME 81
Pussyhat Throw Pillow 83
Pussyhat Pet Bed 87
Luscious Lounge Slippers 97
Needle Felted Wool Coasters 101
Quilted Mug Rug 105
Well Read Bookmarks 109
Girl Power Knitted Bath Mitt and Washcloth 113
Pussyhat Holiday Ornament 117
Resist Felted Rug 121
Resistance Ornaments 127

AROUND TOWN 131

HeForShe Coffee Cup Cozy 133
Resistance Cowl 137
Pussyhat Bombs 141
Jabot-Inspired Scarf 145
Nasty Nag Pouch 149
Yellow Rose Pin 159
Free-Range Pussyhat Symbols 163
Purple Reins of Power Scarf 169
Don't Be Ladylike Cowl 173

ABBREVIATIONS 175
CONTRIBUTORS 176
BIBLIOGRAPHY 178
SOME OF OUR FAVORITE ORGANIZATIONS AND RESOURCES 180

Emancipation should make it possible for women to be human in the truest sense. Everything within her that craves assertion and activity should reach its fullest expression; all artificial barriers should be broken, and the road towards greater freedom cleared of every trace of centuries of submission and slavery.

—Emma Goldman, 1912

INTRODUCTIONS

I'm a lifelong crafter. I've dabbled in (and been addicted to) knitting, needle felting, spinning, weaving, and sewing. I love them all, for different reasons. Primarily, I agree with Annie Modesitt, who reminds us that crafters create to make themselves happy, not because they think they need more stuff.

I also take great joy in teaching others how to knit and explore other creative pursuits. Often, the upcoming arrival of a baby provides a reason to take up the needles. In the past, knitting and sewing projects were taken on to help support war efforts. Today is no different, really, except that we are the troops and we use words instead of guns to fight for our cause.

I recently read Gloria Steinem's *My Life on the Road.* It's a wonderful, complex book. Steinem was a contemporary, friend, and confidant of Wilma Mankiller. I was too young to vote, but I had the good fortune of being at least a little politically aware when Mankiller was reelected principal chief of the Cherokee Nation in 1991. As a member of the Cherokee Nation and as a woman, I looked up to Mankiller. Steinem's portrait of her, which includes her death in 2010, is humbling and moving. It also provides a personal detail. Steinem writes, "Among her last requests was that everyone wear or carry something in her improbable favorite color: bright pink."

I've always had a strained relationship with pink. In my mind, it is closely associated with unrealistic fashion dolls, cheaply made underwear from the mall, and entirely too much branding on breast cancer awareness. (I'm all for breast cancer awareness, but it's hard for me not to cast a long side-eye at companies that have harnessed pink ribbons as a marketing ploy without seeming especially interested in reducing cancer rates.)

Before my wife, sister, and I joined the sea of pink at the March for Women in January 2017, I sewed several Pussyhats and wore mine with pride. In private, I worried that I might not wear my hat again. Pink, after all, wasn't "my" color. I'm more of a black-and-gray-and-sometimes-red person.

However, I had a very fun encounter about a week after the March. I was wearing my hat in line at the post office when the lady in front of me told me she liked my hat. She wanted to know where I got it, so I told her I made it, asked her if she had one, and said I would give it to her if she would wear it. She was excited, and I was very happy to be able to give it to her. We decided that my payment should be her simply increasing her usual donation to Planned Parenthood.

I made a little vow to myself. Whenever I had a hat to wear, I would make sure I had at least one in my purse to give away, too. I'm much more comfortable now with bright pink, and I will be even more proud to wear it, since I know that it carries a connection to the person who taught everyone the power of a woman leader in Indian country.

Lara

re•sis•tance /rə'zistəns/ *noun*

1. the refusal to accept or comply with something; the attempt to prevent something by action or argument.
   "She **put up** no **resistance to** being led away."

2. the ability not to be affected by something, especially adversely.
   "Some of us have a lower resistance to cold than others."

Resistance is not new. As long as there has been oppression, there has been resistance and advocates for justice. There are countless examples of inequality and oppression from societies all around the world and throughout the historical record.

But there have also been movements. Look at the abolition of apartheid in South Africa, the indigenous rights movements of native peoples worldwide, and, in the United States, the abolition of slavery, the fight for women's suffrage, and the Civil Rights Movement.

All of these movements have one thing in common. A group of people see injustice and they organize to fight it and change it, no matter how long that fight takes. Sometimes that fight goes on for decades. What is needed to keep the movement cohesive and effective is unity and a common message.

Crafters have long been a part of these movements. Just as any artist, we use our creativity to make a statement and to spread the word. Through our art, we educate. We create unity. We spread the message of the movement. The white sashes worn by suffragists in the US and in England are a great example. The Pussyhats worn by activists around the world in the winter and spring of 2017 are another.

This book provides a wealth of different types of projects that can help you continue to spread the word, carry the message, support the cause, spark a conversation! We hope you'll find these projects speak to you and help you carry the message of *your* movement.

With love and solidarity,
Heather

A Very Short History of Craftivism

Betsy Greer coined the term *craftivism* in the early years of the twenty-first century and launched Craftivism.com in 2003. Her short definition is: "Craftivism is a way of looking at life where voicing opinions through creativity makes your voice stronger, your compassion deeper, and your quest for justice more infinite." Her work connects to a long history of handcrafts supporting political causes. For example, spinning bees were organized as part of the break away from England and English goods during the Revolutionary War. Also, Mahatma Gandhi's swadeshi movement relied on the production of goods at home as a path to political, economic, and cultural independence.

The Pussyhat Project exploded onto the world stage in late 2016. Krista Suh and Jayna Zweiman put out the call for a "sea of pink hats" for the Women's March on Washington in January 2017, and knitters, crocheters, and sewists answered it. It was so successful that some opponents questioned its authenticity, expressing disbelief that so many hats could have been handmade in such a short amount of time. To us, this says they've been ignoring our voices for so long that they don't know our numbers, capacity, or dedication.

In many ways and for many reasons, rhetorical domestic tasks have been used against causes for social equality. Conversely, taking on work that is coded as feminine is the ultimate bogeyman for masculinity. If women vote, the argument goes, will men darn the socks? If a woman can be in charge in the government, at work, or over her own finances, who will do the cooking?

Craftivism turns this hand-wringing back on itself. In a just world, anyone can be in charge. Cooking, darning socks, and any other handy skill should be a choice, not an automatic obligation of any gender.

We reject the false dichotomy of our lives being divided into the spheres of "home" vs. "world."

Our home is the world. Watch what we make it.

TIPS AND TRICKS

SEWING

Topstitching will always look better if you choose a longer stitch length. This helps the thread stand out, but it also makes your stitching look straighter. A little wobbling on a line is less obvious when the stitch length is longer.

When topstitching, you may have an urge to watch the needle as you guide your fabric through the machine. This is actually just about the hardest way to do it! Instead, practice on scraps and watch how your other seams line up on parts of your presser foot. If you can, move your needle position to the left or the right and see how that affects your work. If all else fails, there is no shame in using chalk to mark where a seam or topstitched line should fall. Test to make sure your marks will not be permanent.

KNITTING

Swatch. Swatch. Swatch. You hear this all the time and you hate it. You just want to get started on the project already. But trust me, you will really be glad you did swatch when after so many hours you are done with the project and it fits perfectly.

When working stranded colorwork, be sure to pick a hand for each color and *stick with that setup* throughout the entire project. Each of our hands tensions yarn differently. If you knit with white in the right hand and blue in the left one day, or on the first wrister, and blue in the right and white in the left the next, or on the second wrister, the results *will be different*. Pick which color is going in your dominant hand and stick with that for the duration of the project. Not sure you believe me? Test it out for yourself when you swatch. You'll see that whichever yarn you are holding in your dominant hand will be more prominent in the work.

Read the pattern all the way through before starting. This is great advice for cooking and baking too. Mystery knit-alongs are fun, but you can get into trouble if you get halfway through a project and are suddenly facing a technique you've never done. Save yourself the panic and read the pattern first.

SPECIAL TOOLS

By Lara Neel

I had a boss, years ago, who pointed out something to me that I might otherwise not have noticed. Women tend to resist acquiring a tool to complete a project. This habit is even mocked in popular culture. Who hasn't tried to use a shoe instead of a hammer or a butter knife instead of a screwdriver? I'll tell you who—probably not a man. Why? It's not because women are stupid or don't want to do a good job. Maybe it's because we have been taught that our work, no matter if it's sewing, hanging a photograph, or fixing our glasses, isn't worth an investment of money, space, and care.

I'm not saying you have to buy an industrial sewing machine that costs two thousand dollars, but make sure that your equipment is in good shape. Old thread and dull needles take the joy out of any project pretty quickly. When you're getting ready to knit, check to see if the style and size of knitting needles you have will be comfortable for you to use. Personally, I love bamboo needles when I knit afghans, but I would struggle to make socks with anything but my beloved steel double-pointed needles.

BASIC SEWING KIT

These are the supplies that I consider essential to sewing almost any project.

Sewing machine in good working order

- Get yours checked out and professionally cleaned if it has been in storage for over a year. Servicing a machine is usually much cheaper than buying a new one.
- If you don't have one, start asking around. You'll be surprised at how many people you know used to sew and no longer do. You may even pick up a mentor in the process!

Bobbins for the sewing machine

- Different machines use different sizes and shapes of bobbins. Check the manual to make sure you have the correct kind.

Sewing machine needles

- Use ball point for knits and regular point for wovens. I like to buy multisize packs of needles so that I can experiment with the needle size.
- Change your needle often, especially when working with tough materials, synthetics, and fleece.

Straight pins

- I use ball point for knits and regular point for wovens.

Wonder clips or binder clips

- Wonder clips are one of those tools that were first designed for quilters, but now sewists of all kinds are discovering them. I use them more often than pins! I find them faster to use. If you don't want to invest in them, sometimes binder clips from the office supply store will work, too.

Thread

- I use all-purpose polyester thread for most applications.
- If you don't have thread that matches, try a shade of gray. It won't be perfect, but it sometimes blends well enough in a pinch.
- If you are choosing between two colors that almost match your project, pick the darker color. If the thread color is lighter than your project, it will stand out more.

Marking tools

- There is a broad range of choices for marking fabric, and one tool won't work for every project. When in doubt, test on a scrap. Check to see if the marks you make will stay clear enough to be useful and still come out when you are finished.
- My favorite options are chalk markers, water-erasable pens, and Scotch tape, depending on the project's material.

Hand-sewing needles

- You want to have several sizes on hand.

Ruler
Measuring tape
Shears
Rotary cutter and self-healing mat
Iron and an ironing board
Seam ripper

BEYOND THE BASIC SEWING TOOLS

These aren't as essential as items in the basic kit, but they are nice to have and will make your sewing time more productive.

Walking Foot

- A walking foot helps thick, bulky layers feed more evenly through your sewing machine. It's invaluable when working with fleece.

Tailor's clapper

- A tailor's clapper is made of hardwood. The best ones are shaped to fit your hand well.

Sleeve ironing board

- This tiny ironing board makes pressing any small area much easier.

Hump jumper

- Helps you cross over bulky seams without breaking needles or suffering skipped stitches. Hitting a heavy seam with a hammer is a good start, but sometimes you need a little extra help on top of that.

Iron finger

- It looks like a giant blue finger. I love mine for pressing just about any tight spot. It's also great for pushing corners out until they are sharp.

Hemostats

- Yes, the surgical tools. They're affordable and great for gripping threads. I find them invaluable when threading a serger or ripping out stitches.

PATTERNMAKING SUPPLIES AND TRACING OR PHOTOCOPYING MATERIALS

A few of the patterns in this book are too large to fit on one page. For those, we have included a dashed line along one edge, which indicates that only half of the pattern piece is represented. To make full pattern pieces, either photocopy the pattern twice and tape the pieces together along the dashed line; or trace the piece, then fold your paper along the dashed line to trace and cut out the other side.

Paper

- Any kind of paper will do for making paper patterns. I've even used taped-together printer paper when I didn't have any other options. The easiest paper to use for tracing or making patterns is Swedish tracing paper. It's tough enough to stitch through, but relatively transparent, which makes tracing easier.

Tape

- Micropore Surgical Tape by 3M is great for taping together any kind of paper to make larger pieces.

Scissors

- I prefer to use either very cheap scissors or an old rotary cutter and a self-healing mat to cut paper. Paper dulls blades much faster than fabric, so you don't want to mix up your patternmaking cutting tools with the ones you use for fabric.

Yardstick

- A yardstick from the hardware store can be your best friend. It makes cutting square and rectangular pieces of paper and fabric a snap.

KNITTING TOOLS

Like most knitters, I tend to collect tools and yarn. The great thing about a stash is it's always there when you need it! Many of the knitting projects in this book require very little yarn, so what is already in your stash may work perfectly. Just be sure to swatch! When substituting yarn in a pattern, swatching is crucial. A basic 6" x 6" swatch done in stockinette stitch on the needles of your choice will suffice to check the gauge listed in the pattern.

If you measure for gauge and get more stitches per inch than the pattern recommends, that means your knitting is too tight. Simply go up a needle size and try again. (I'm a tight knitter so I *always* just start out two needle sizes bigger and I'm usually right on gauge.)

TIP!

To save time, I cast on my swatch in the needle size recommended and knit the swatch for four inches, then switch to a bigger needle size (because I always knit tighter), knit another four inches, then switch to a bigger needle, knit another four inches, then bind off. I put a few rows of garter stitch in between each section as I go. Then you can measure three different sizes to find the right gauge.

If you measure for gauge and you get fewer stitches per inch than the pattern recommends, your knitting is too loose and you can simply go down a needle size.

Sometimes you just can't get gauge no matter how many needle sizes you try. In that case, the problem is most likely the yarn you are using. Be sure to use the same yarn weight as the pattern recommends when substituting yarns. If you still can't get gauge (this has only happened to me a few times in many years), then you need to try a different yarn.

Needles—flat or circular? This is often dictated by the project but sometimes just by choice. I knit everything, whether flat or in the round, with my circular needles. I just find them less cumbersome and more ergonomic for my hands. The wristers in the book can be knitted with double-pointed needles, two circulars, or one large circular using magic loop. The choice is yours.

BASIC KNITTER'S TOOL KIT

- **Set of needles in multiple sizes.** The most common ones are sizes US 6–8.
- **Small scissors**
- **Tapestry needles**
- **Gauge guide.** To help measure for gauge.
- **Small tape measure**
- **Set of bobbins**. For use in intarsia projects.
- **Stitch markers, both locking and round**. These can be fun and *very* useful.

Here are extra items that are not necessary, but some folks find them helpful.

- **A full set of interchangeable circular needles.** I have one of these and I use it *all the time*. Different size cables plus the whole range of needle sizes. Pricey but a great investment.
- **Blocking mats.** These are very helpful to pin down projects, especially lace projects, to the perfect shape when blocking. I don't have one. I just use a thick towel and straight pins.

- **Yarn ball winder and yarn swift.** Not essential, but I highly recommend these. Many yarns now come as skeins, not balls, so you have to wind your own. A yarn ball winder expedites that process and saves you from a lot of knotting and headaches. Plus, it produces a center pull ball so you don't have your yarn rolling all over the floor. If you have a swift, then that can hold your skein in perfect tension while you wind onto the ball winder. I have both and love them. Then again, if you have a willing helper, you can do it the old-fashioned way, using their arms to hold the skein as you wind.
- **Project bags.** These can get pricey. It is great to have an individual bag for each of your WIPs (works in progress) but it isn't necessary to fork over cold, hard cash for them. I use the many totes I already have lying around or just plain gallon-size ziplock bags.
- **Yarn stranding guide.** This is a little gizmo that you wear on your finger to help hold the various strands of yarn when you are working with multiple colors. It supposedly keeps them orderly. I don't use one, but some folks swear by them.
- **Row counters.** These are little devices that you can either wear on your finger or keep next to you and you click each time you finish a row or round to keep track of where you are. I don't have one. I either just use a Post-it and a pencil and keep track with hash marks, or I use an app in my phone called Knitting Bag Simple where I can track row, gauge, repeat, etc., for every project. You can even take photos of this project in the app.

I want full freedom and cooperation to evolve as a human being, to gain wisdom and knowledge. To be sure, I want certain rights guaranteed to me, not because I am a woman, but because I am a human being.

—Elinor Gene Knudsen Hoffman

ON THE MARCH

Clarity Vinyl Tote

by Lara Neel

Experience Level: Advanced Beginner, because of the materials used

Completely see-through bags are an unfortunate necessity in the modern age. Many schools, sporting events, and protests suggest or require them to speed up security screenings. Vinyl is easier to sew than you might think. With a few simple tools and some webbing, you'll be whipping up these bags in no time.

Pair this bag with 1984 by George Orwell. Big Brother can look all he wants. Let him see our resistance!

MATERIALS

½ yard of vinyl

Self-healing mat and rotary cutter

Notions

Basic sewing kit

4 yards of 1-inch webbing for straps

All-purpose thread that matches your webbing

Leather or jeans needle

Walking foot, Teflon foot, or roller foot

Zipper foot

Wonder clips or binder clips

Zipper at least 19 inches long (see Tips)

Washaway Wonder Tape

Leather tape (optional)

China marker or grease pencil (optional)

FINISHED MEASUREMENTS

9.5" x 18" (height x width)

SKILLS NEEDED

You should be comfortable using a sewing machine and cutting out projects using a rotary cutter and mat.

Scotch tape

TIPS

- Vinyl doesn't have a nap or direction, so cutting out is fairly simple. Cut your pieces however they fit best. You need to use a rotary cutter and mat. It will be difficult to cut accurately with scissors.
- Test your machine to see how heavy a vinyl it can handle. Buy the smallest samples you can of two or three different weights and practice stitching plain seams and topstitching. I ended up using 20 gauge vinyl, but a thinner material would still work well. Be sure to test your needles, tensions, and stitch length. When a project is totally see-through, there's literally no place to hide, so take the extra time to make sure everything is just right before you start.

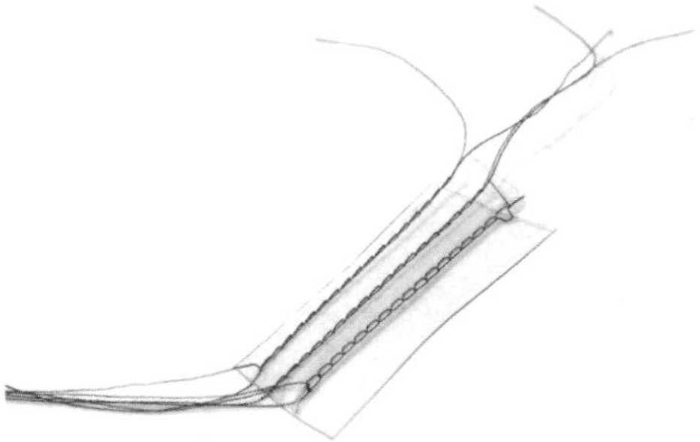

- I like the heavyweight style of zipper for this bag. The zipper tape should measure 1¼ inches across. If it doesn't, you may have to adjust the length of the zipper end cover.
- Choose a longer stitch length than usual, as shorter stitches will actually make your vinyl weaker. I used a 3.5 mm length for seams and 4 mm for topstitching.
- Do not use pins! Pin marks are permanent in vinyl. Use wonder clips or binder clips.
- Vinyl is very stiff, so you'll want to clear off the workspace around your sewing machine. I got a bit stuck on one of my seams and it took me a few minutes to realize that the problem was a little odd—the end of my bag was hitting a stack of books on the other side of my kitchen table!
- Chalk marking won't work on vinyl. Scotch tape and Post-it notes can work as markers. However, test and make sure that the adhesive from the tape comes off your vinyl. Some tapes and some vinyls don't want to ever let go of each other, and that can be frustrating. You could also try using a china marker to mark your vinyl. Again, test to see if it will resist removal.

CUTTING INSTRUCTIONS

Cut two lengths of webbing, 63 inches long, for the straps.

Cut another piece of webbing, 3¼ inches long, for the zipper end cover.

Cut two sides for your bag out of vinyl: 12¾ inches tall and 19 inches wide. (see Tips)

INSTRUCTIONS

1. Secure the top end of the zipper with Scotch tape and unzip it, to give yourself room to work.

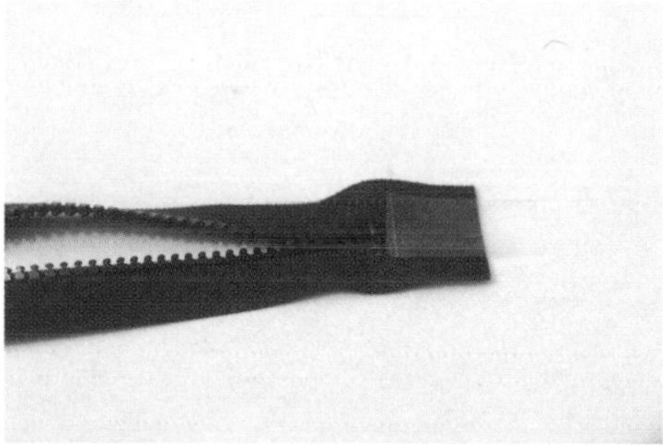

2. Stitch the zipper end cover into a loop with a ½-inch seam allowance. Turn the loop right-side out.

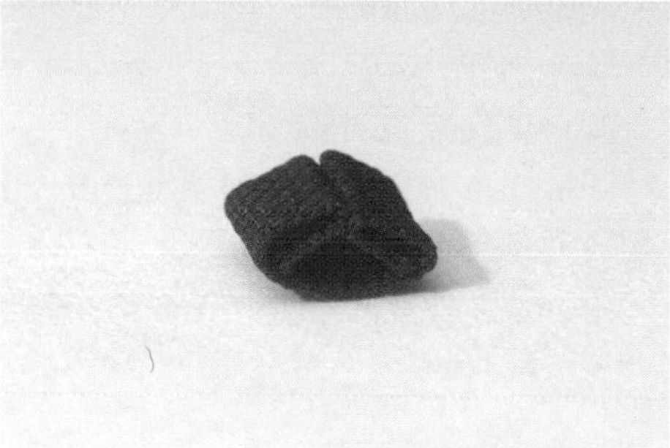

3. Using a zipper foot, stitch the cover to the end of the zipper. It should be a snug fit.

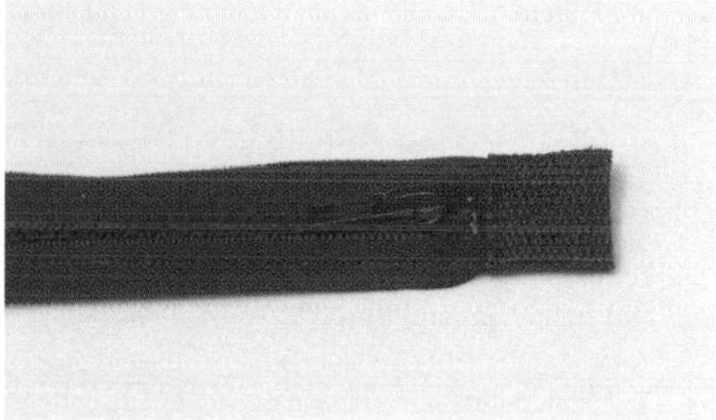

4. Choose which long sides of your bag will be the top edges. Mark ½ inch from each end with your method of choice. I used a Post-it note.

   Line up the edge of the zipper teeth with these positioning marks on the top edge of the bag.

5. Prepare your zipper foot by covering the bottom of it with Scotch tape and trimming away any excess tape. This will help keep the vinyl from sticking as you stitch.

6. With the underside of the zipper facing up, line up the edge of your finished zipper end with the mark you placed in step 4. Stitch the zipper in place, stitching close to the zipper teeth, with the vinyl on top and the zipper tape on the bottom. Stop stitching at the mark on the other end of the bag. If your zipper is longer than 19 inches, allow any extra length to simply hang off the end of the bag.

7. Turn the bag around and attach the other side of the zipper to the other side of the bag in the same way.

8. Topstitch both sides of the zipper tape in place, as close to the outer edge of the zipper tape as possible.

9. Unzip the zipper and lay the bag out, flat, right-side up. Along the bottom edges, measure 5 inches in and use clips to attach one strap to each side. Make sure that the straps aren't twisted or crossed.

10. Move the zipper pull so that it is halfway across the top of the bag. Fold the bag, right sides together. With a walking foot, Teflon foot, or roller foot, stitch the sides and bottom in one long seam with a ½-inch seam allowance. It can be difficult to maintain the seam allowance when you are close to the zipper teeth, but just do your best. When you stitch over the straps on the bottom seam, you will have a lot of thick material to go through, so work slowly and consider using the handwheel on your machine to "walk" the needle over those areas. I like to increase my stitch length even more for those areas.

11. If your webbing seems as if it will fray a lot, stitch the ends of the webbing down to the seam allowance of the bottom of the bag, using a zipper foot.

12. Carefully cut the corners to, but not through, the stitching line.

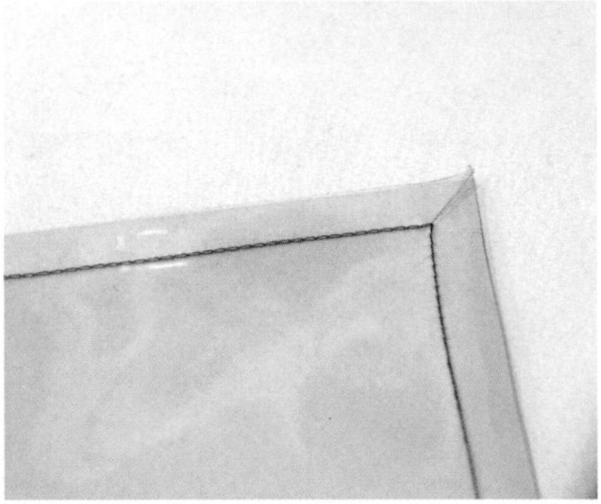

13. With your fingers, push the seam allowances so that they lie open. They may not lie perfectly flat, but get them as flat as possible. Pinch the corner on the bottom of the bag so that it is flat and mark a line that is 3 inches away from the corner. Stitch along that line, perpendicular to the bottom seam. Do not backstitch.

Instead, gently pull on the bobbin thread to bring the needle thread through to the same side as the bobbin thread, then tie the two threads in a knot. Trim close to the knot. Repeat on the other side.

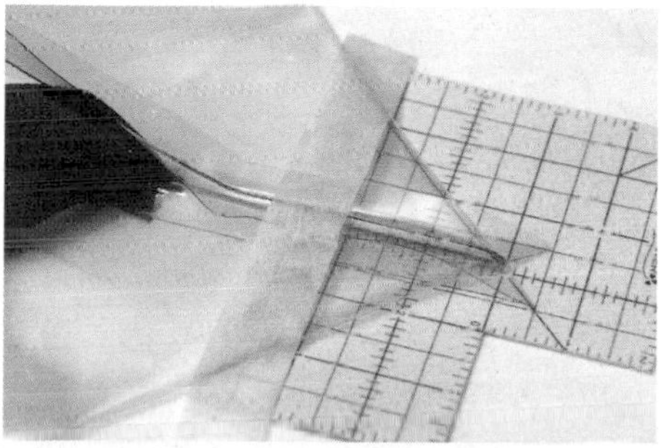

14. Carefully turn your bag right-side out. This may take a little persistence, but slow and steady pressure should do the trick.

15. Stand your bag up and decide where you want the straps to attach to the zipper tape. I used Washaway Wonder Tape to baste the straps in place, but hand-basting would also work. Stitch in place.

16. (Optional) Use leather tape to secure the inner corners of the bag to the bottom.

Go Anywhere, Say Anything Messenger Bag

by Lara Neel

Experience Level: Intermediate

This little bag is roughly the size that was suggested for nonsee-through bags at the Women's March on Washington in 2017. It's basically a tiny messenger bag, but there is a zipper in the lining, so you can zip it up to make it more secure when needed. It's "Go Anywhere" because it should be good to go in almost any setting. It's "Say Anything" because the cloth flap easily holds buttons, pins, and badges.

I wear messenger bags as purses a great deal, and the little-sister size of this one made me laugh out loud when I made it. However, when I put my (unnecessarily) large wallet, phone, keys, and small zippered bag inside it, I stopped laughing. All of my daily essentials fit into this little bag! It has now become my everyday purse.

There are a lot of benefits to having a just-big-enough bag. I don't have to paw around in it to look for things. I can see at a glance what I have in there. I also don't have to resist the urge to cram a bunch of extra stuff into my bag. As an added benefit, no one has asked me to hold their keys/sunglasses/wallet in my bag. They clearly won't fit. This bag says: "Carry your own stuff."

MATERIALS

1 yard of main fabric (see Tips)

½ yard of lining fabric (see Tips)

1 yard of woven sew-in interfacing (I used Pellon's SF785)

Notions

Matching all-purpose thread

Zipper that is at least 14 inches long

Hammer

A surface you feel comfortable hammering (I use my tailor's clapper, but a thick book would work, too.)

A pair of scissors for trimming zipper tape (see Tips)

Zipper foot

Walking foot (optional)

Basic sewing kit

Jeans needle

Sewing needle to match the thickness of your lining fabric

Set of two 2-inch D-rings

Washaway Wonder Tape (optional)

Patternmaking supplies or photocopier

FINISHED MEASUREMENTS

8" x 5.5" x 5" (width x height x depth)

CUTTING INSTRUCTIONS

To conserve fabric, fold your lining fabric and cut 2 pieces of the zippered lining, part 2 (page 26), near the selvedge edge. Unfold your fabric. Cut 2 pieces of the zippered lining, part 1 (page 25), from the center of your fabric. Then, cut out the flap (page 23) however it fits best on your fabric.

From the main fabric, cut two outer bag pieces (page 24), one flap (page 23), and the straps (see below).
Cut interfacing pieces for straps.

Pieces without patterns:

- Strap 1, from main fabric: 5" x 8.5"
- Strap 2, from main fabric: 5" x 38"
- Strap 1, from woven sew-in interfacing: 2" x 6.5"
- Strap 2, from woven sew-in interfacing: 2" x 36"

TIP!

Patterns with a dashed line along one edge indicates that only half of the pattern piece is represented. To make full pattern pieces, either photocopy the pattern twice and tape the pieces together along the dashed line; or trace the piece, then fold your paper along the dashed line to trace and cut out the other side.

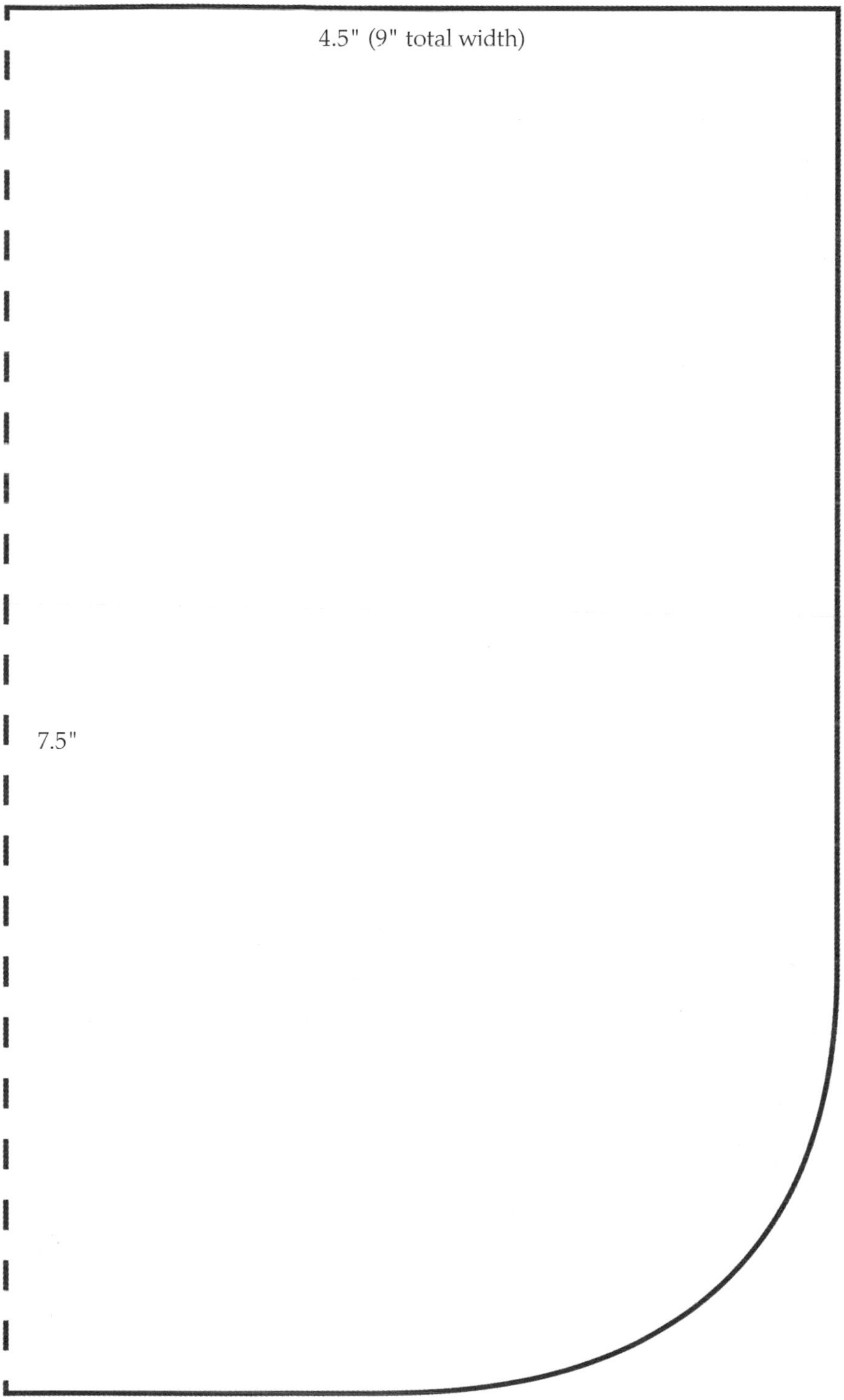

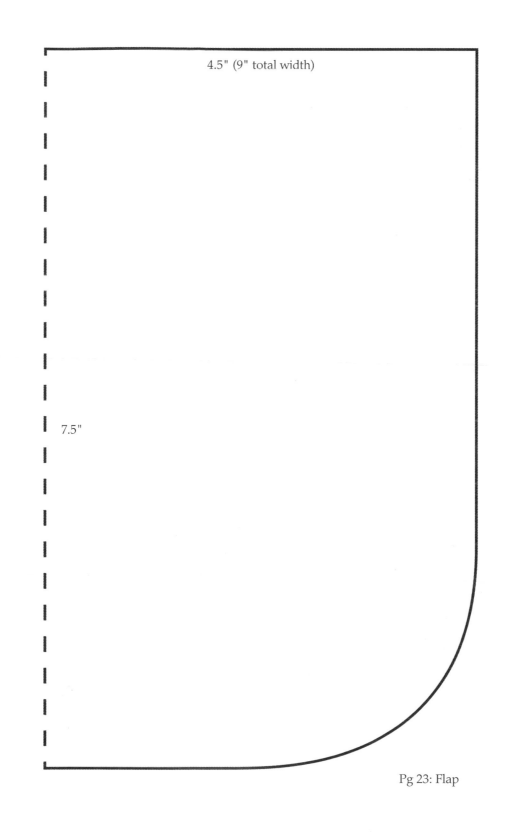

Pg 23: Flap

6.5" (13" total width)
9"
2.5"
2.5"
Pg 24: Outer bag

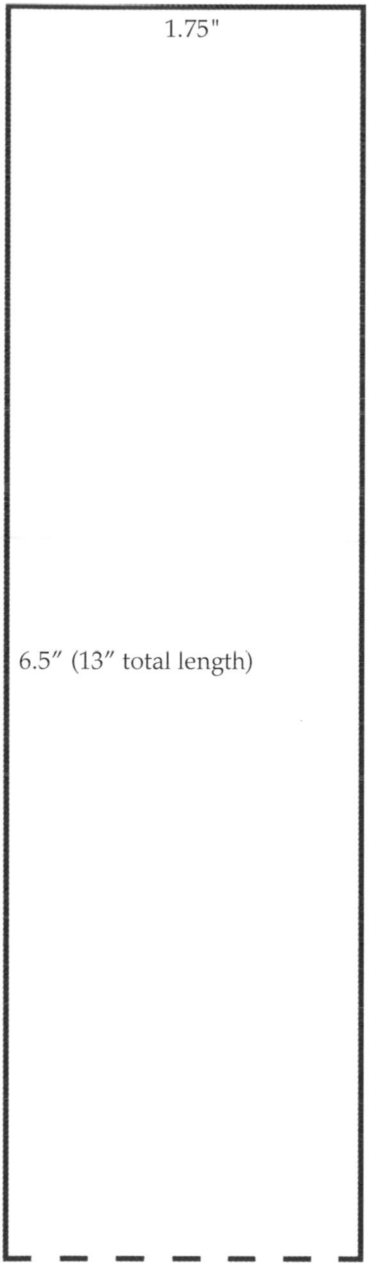

Pg 25: Zippered lining, part 1

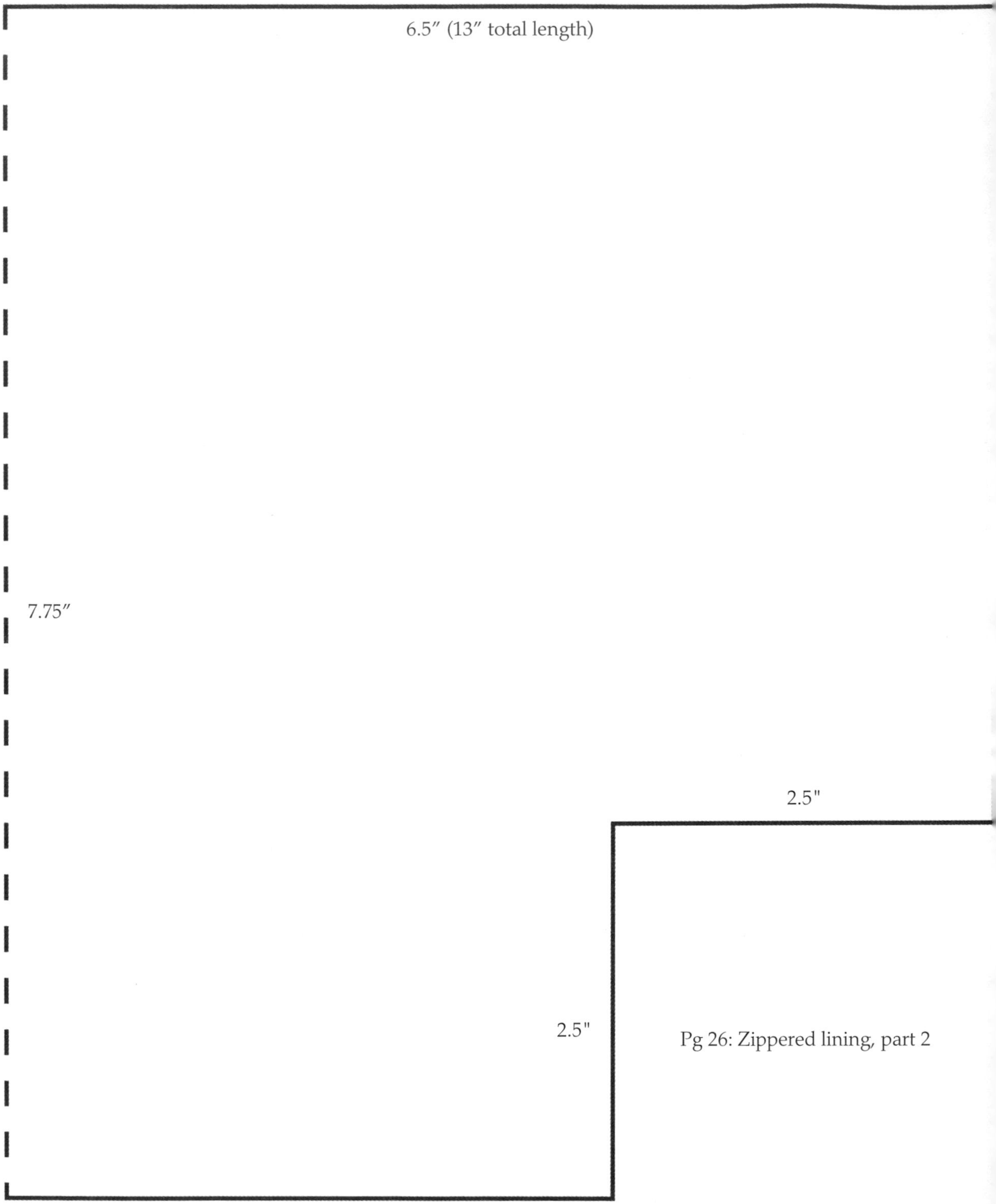
6.5″ (13″ total length)
7.75″
2.5"
2.5"
Pg 26: Zippered lining, part 2

TIPS

- For the main fabric, I used heavy 100% cotton canvas that I found in the outdoor fabrics section of the fabric store.
- For lining fabric, use any fabric you like, but try to find one that has almost no stretch at all. Many shirting fabrics have lovely colors and a nice drape, but are designed to stretch. Stitching a stretch fabric to a non-stretch zipper tape can be too big a challenge to be worth the effort.
- I used cotton quilting fabric for my lining. These pattern pieces will fit on fabric that is as narrow as 42 inches wide. If your fabric has a print on it, especially if it looks different when rotated, you may need more fabric.
- When it comes to topstitching the strap, in my opinion, consistency between the lines of topstitching counts for more than how evenly those lines align with the outer edges of the strap. I decided to align the outer edge of my walking foot with each previous line of stitching as I worked. I ended up with 6 lines that were slightly over ¼ inch apart from each other. My first line of stitching was about ⅛ inch away from the edge. I "lost" about ⅛ inch to the thickness of the strap from turning the cloth at the fold. All of that means that my very last line of stitching was a little less than ¼ inch from the outer edge of the strap. I'm perfectly happy with that, but if any irregularity bothers you, please make yourself an extra mini-strap and test your topstitching widths until you are happy with them. Don't forget to use a little interfacing in your test piece, as that may affect your results.
- Using a zipper that is longer than the pattern pieces allows you to move the zipper slider out of the way as you work. Since the ends of the zipper tape will be encased between the lining and the main bag, it's very easy to simply trim away excess zipper tape once you have stitched the sides of the lining together. Do not use your sewing shears to trim the zipper. Any old pair of scissors will do.

INSTRUCTIONS

1. Press each strap piece's long edge in by ½ inch.
2. Press your strap pieces in half, lengthwise.
3. Tuck your interfacing pieces inside the straps. They will most likely stick out at least a little bit; measure how much. Remove the interfacing pieces from the straps and trim by that amount.

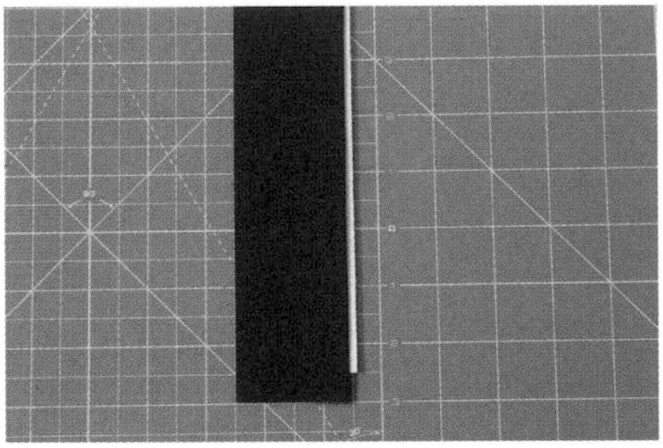

4. Lay your straps out, with the open edges toward you and the short strap on the left and the long strap on the right. Place your interfacing pieces inside the straps, ½ inch from the left raw edge for the short strap and ½ inch from the right raw edge for the long strap. This will leave 1½ inches on the other ends of the straps without interfacing. Pin or clip the straps closed. With either a pin or a wonder clip, mark the short sides of the straps that have 1½ inches between the end of the interfacing and the end of the strap.
5. If you have a walking foot, use it. Using your jeans needle, stitch close to the open edge of the straps. On the short strap, start at the marked short end. On the long strap, start at the unmarked short end. Keep the top of each strap facing up as you stitch.
6. Topstitch either 4 or 5 more times along each strap, always working in the same direction, to reduce the chance of ripples (see Tips).
7. Place your long strap underside up and remove the marking pin or clip from the marked short end. Press that short end up by about ¼ inch and pound it with your hammer. Turn it on itself, again, so that all raw edges are enclosed. Press it, then pound it with your hammer. Stitch it in position.
8. Place your short strap top-side up and repeat the same process of finishing the strap end.
9. Switch to a zipper foot and the correct needle for your lining fabric. Lay out one zippered lining, part 2 (page 26), faceup. Center the zipper over that piece, faceup. Lay a zippered lining, part 1 (page 25), facedown on them both, aligning the zipper tape with the raw edges

of the lining pieces. Stitch through all layers.

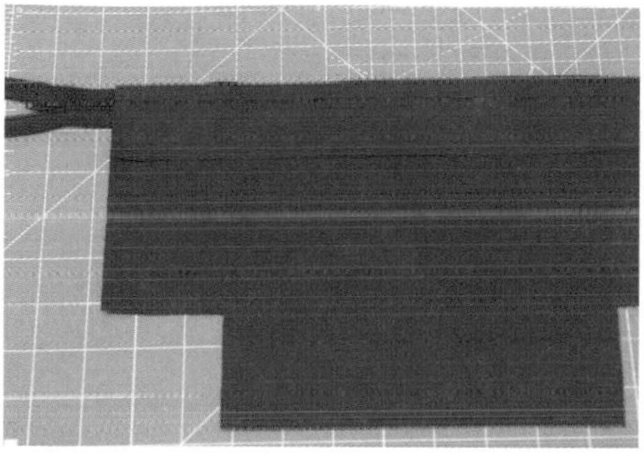

10. Press the two parts of the lining away from the zipper, taking care not to touch the zipper teeth with the iron.

11. Line up the second side of the zippered lining pieces with the other side of the zipper, just as you did for the first side. Stitch through all layers.

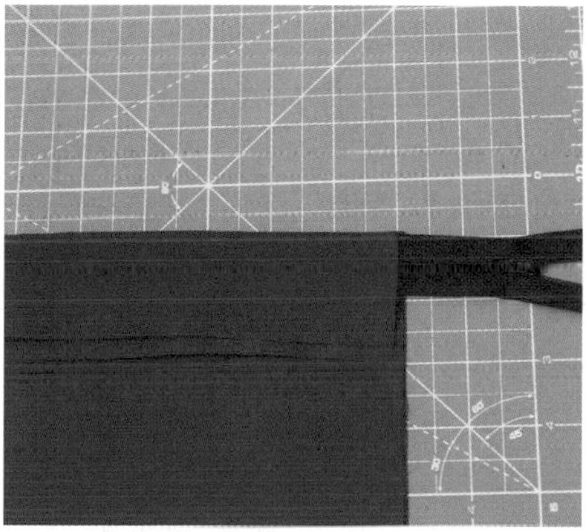

12. Press the lining away from the zipper, taking care not to touch the zipper tape with the iron.

13. Move your zipper slider to the middle of the lining. With a regular foot, stitch the sides and the bottom of the lining closed, with a ½-inch seam allowance. Work slowly when stitching over the zipper teeth. Leaving an inch or two on both sides, trim away excess zipper tape. Press the seams open.

14. On one corner, bring the end of the side seam and the end of the bottom seam together. Stitch across this bottom corner, with a ½-inch seam allowance. Repeat on the other side.

15. Switch to the jeans needle. With the right sides together, stitch the flap lining to the outer bag flap with a ½-inch seam allowance, leaving the straight edge open. Trim away half of the seam allowance. Cut notches in the seam allowances at the curved edges.

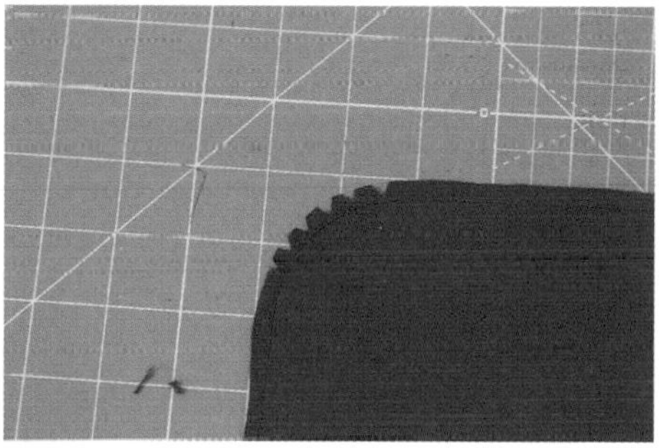

16. Turn the flap right-side out, press, and topstitch ¼ inch from the edge. Leave the straight edge open.

17. With the right sides together, stitch the two sides of the outer bag with a ½-inch seam allowance, then stitch across the bottom of the bag. Press the seams open.

18. On one corner, bring the end of the side seam and the end of the bottom seam together. Use a pin to make sure that the two seam allowances are lined up perfectly. Stitch across this bottom corner, with a ½-inch seam allowance. Repeat on the other side.

19. Turn the outer bag right-side out. With the right sides together, center the flap on one side of the bag and baste it in place.

20. With the flap side of the bag toward you, center the raw edge of the short strap over the left-side seam of the bag. Make sure that the top side of the strap is against the bag and the stitched edge of the strap is facing you. The folded edge of the strap is facing away from you. Baste the strap into place.

21. With the flap side of the bag toward you, center the raw edge of the long strap over the right side seam of the bag. Make sure that the top side of the strap is against the bag and the stitched edge of the strap is facing you. The folded edge of the strap is facing away from you. Baste the strap into place.

22. Turn the outer bag inside out and tuck the straps and flap into it.

23. Turn the lining right-side out and place it inside the outer bag. If you have an opinion about which side of the bag your zipper pull should face, place the lining so that the pull is on the opposite side of its final position. The lining and the main bag are now right sides together, so everything you can see is the inside of the bag. Press about 5 inches in the center of the front of the main bag down by ½ inch. Press the front of the lining away from the main bag, also by ½ inch, in the same location. Clip or pin the bag and the lining together.

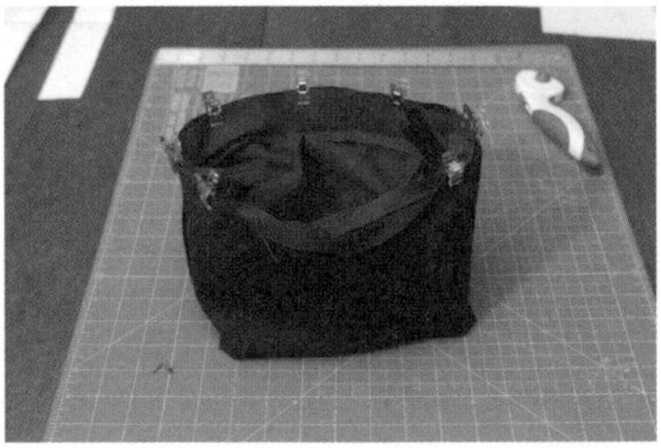

24. Stitch along the top of the bag using a ½-inch seam allowance, leaving the portions you pressed open unstitched. For small circumferences like this, I like to work from the inside of the circle, stitching slowly and rearranging my work frequently. Turn the bag right-side out through the unstitched opening. Press well.

25. If desired, use Washaway Wonder Tape to close the opening in the front of the bag.

26. Topstitch around the top of the bag, as close to the edge as you can. Work very slowly and increase your stitch length in the bulky areas near the outer edges. You may need to use your handwheel to "walk" the needle over them. A walking foot makes this step easier.

27. Fold your long strap end over the two D-rings. Stitch as close to the rings as you can, without striking them. Add another line of stitching as close to that line as you can for added strength.

28. Thread the short strap end through the D-rings and adjust to your desired length.

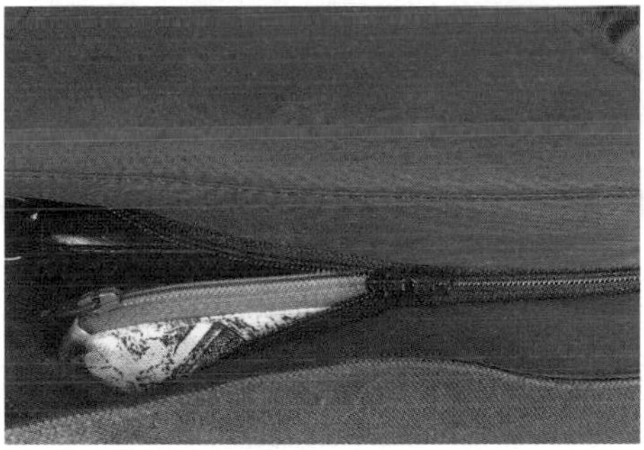

Nasty

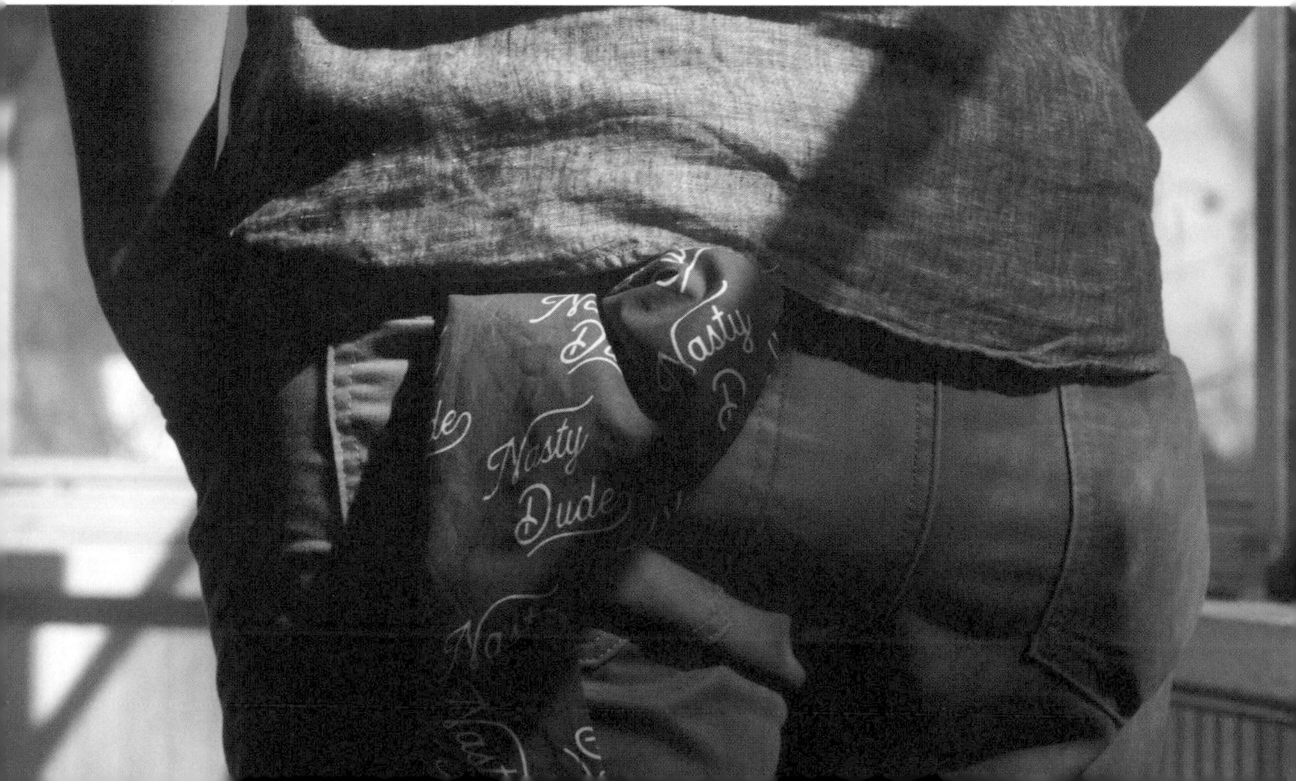
Nasty
Nasty
Dude

Five Unbranded Bandannas

by Lara Neel
Experience Level: Beginner to Intermediate

Bandannas are important for when you are on the march. Of course, you can use them as napkins or handkerchiefs. Once you get used to having one or two on hand, they start to operate like a towel in *The Hitchhiker's Guide to the Galaxy*. However, they can also help reduce the effects of tear gas and other nonlethal crowd control propellants. Wet your bandanna down with water and use it to cover or wipe your face. Don't wear contact lenses if there is any chance at all that you will be in this situation. It ruins the contacts anyway, and is extremely painful for you, too.

Check out The Woman's Dictionary of Symbols and Sacred Objects *by Barbara G. Walker if you don't already have a phrase or message you want to broadcast. Among knitters, Barbara is best known for her pivotal treasuries of knitting patterns, but she has a wonderful, broad body of writing on feminist topics that are just as revolutionary.*

Each of these five bandannas employs a different technique. The first one is the most simple—purchase a plain bandanna and emblazon it with your message! The other four use various methods and range from testing the waters of satin stitch to using a serger for a professional-looking (and very fast) edge.

TOP LEFT: Worn by Dee Milroy
TOP RIGHT: Worn by Maxine Behm
BOTTOM: Worn by Jon Behm

The Nasty Woman and Nasty Dude prints were designed by Caroline Okun. The Resist Pussyhat Pussycat print was designed by Donna Druchunas. If you'd like to use these fabrics, you can purchase them on Spoonflower.com. I chose their Basic Cotton Ultra base for these projects.

You might have noticed white bandannas showing up on fashion runways and the #tiedtogether hashtag. Only time will tell if the white bandanna becomes a universal call for solidarity, but, no matter what, bandannas are pretty darn practical, so there's no harm in having a few extra around.

FINISHED MEASUREMENTS

20" x 20", or the size that fits your fabric the best (see Tips).

TIPS

Spoonflower's Basic Cotton Ultra fabric's printable area is 42 inches wide, but it may shrink by about 4 percent, which brings it closer to 40 inches wide. If you want to get the most out of your yardage, slice off the unprinted selvedge edges. These are great for testing your machine settings. Cut your bandannas at exactly half of the width of your printed fabric, then cut the length so that they are square. Your final products might be a little smaller than the original design, but you will be happier with that than having a lot of wasted fabric. You should be able to make 2 bandannas from one yard of fabric, 4 from 1½ yards of fabric (check with your source, not everyone sells fabric by the half yard), and 6 from 2 yards of fabric.

Satin-Stitch Hemming

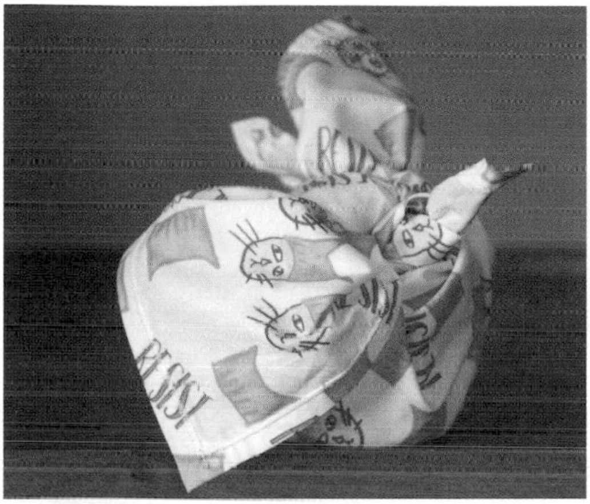

MATERIALS

1 yard of fabric

Notions

Basic sewing kit

Matching all-purpose thread

Satin stitch or open-toe foot

CUTTING INSTRUCTIONS

Cut a piece of fabric that measures 21" x 21".

INSTRUCTIONS

1. Press all of the edges in by ½ inch.

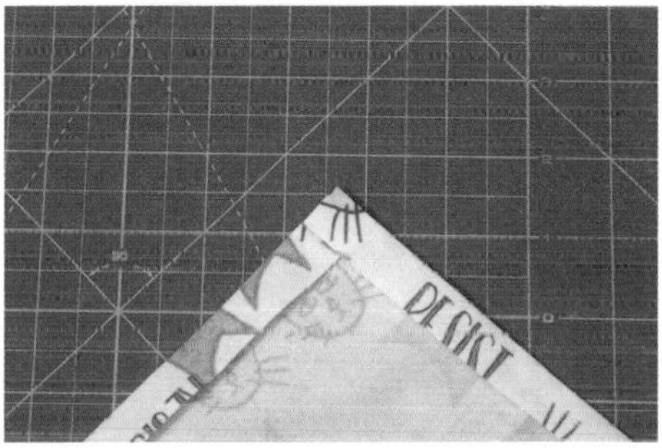

2. Tuck down each corner at the fold line.

3. Fold the raw edges at the corners into miters.

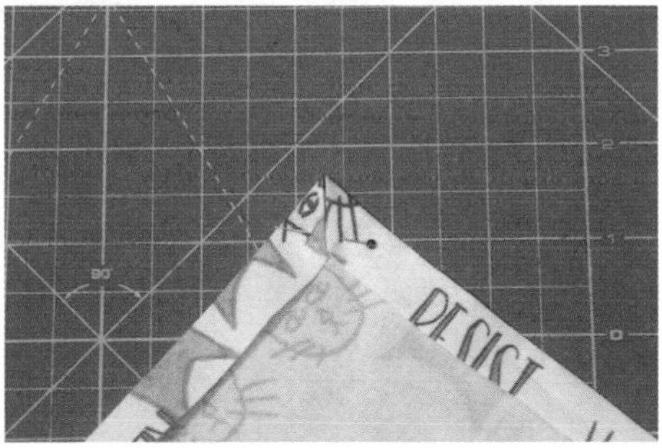

4. Optional: Using a regular stitch length, stitch all the way around, close to the raw edge. You can skip this step, but it helps maintain confidence that the edge won't get away from you on the last step.

5. Switch to satin stitch foot. Stitch all of the way around, ½ inch from the folded edge, with the shortest, widest zigzag stitch that you can manage.

6. Carefully trim away any stray raw edges from the back of your work.

No Hemming or Sewing

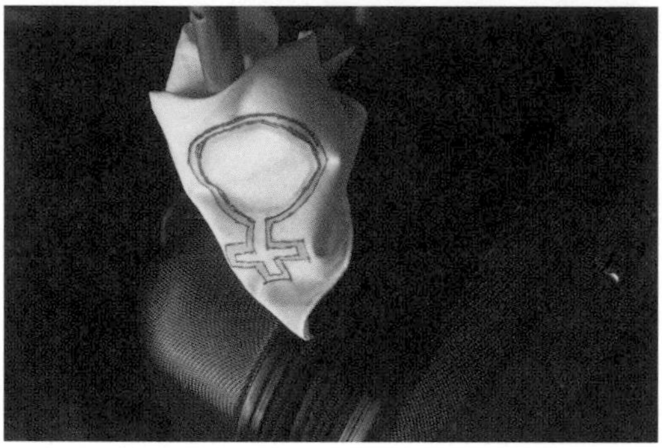

MATERIALS

One purchased bandanna

Iron-on transfer pen

Tracing paper

Permanent fabric marker

INSTRUCTIONS

1. Use the iron-on transfer pen to trace the Venus symbol template (page 39) onto tracing paper.
2. Following the instructions that came with your pen, transfer the symbol onto your bandanna.

3. Trace the transfer using a permanent fabric marker.

Pg 39: Venus symbol

Quarter-Inch Hem

MATERIALS

1 yard of fabric

Notions

Basic sewing kit

Matching all-purpose thread

CUTTING INSTRUCTIONS

Cut a piece of fabric that measures 21" x 21".

Worn by Jeremiah Cheney

INSTRUCTIONS

1. Press all of the edges in by ½ inch.
2. Fold each raw edge until it meets the first pressed crease. Press again.
3. Unfold and turn a corner down along the outer pressed crease. Line up the pressed creases on the edge with the pressed creases on the body of your bandanna.

4. Trim away the corner, from crease mark to crease mark.

5. Fold one side of the miter down.

6. Fold down the other side.

7. Repeat on the other three corners.

8. Stitch all the way around, close to the folded edge. You may find this easier if you move your needle to the right. This allows the entire width of your hem to cover both feed dogs on your machine.

Narrow Hem

MATERIALS

1 yard of fabric

Notions

Basic sewing kit

Matching all-purpose thread

CUTTING INSTRUCTIONS

Cut a piece of fabric that measures 20.5" x 20.5".

Worn by Maxine Behm

INSTRUCTIONS

1. Stitch all the way around the fabric, ¼ inch from the raw edge.

2. Turn each edge so that the stitching line falls just to the back side of the work. Press.

3. Fold each raw edge until it meets the first pressed crease. Press.

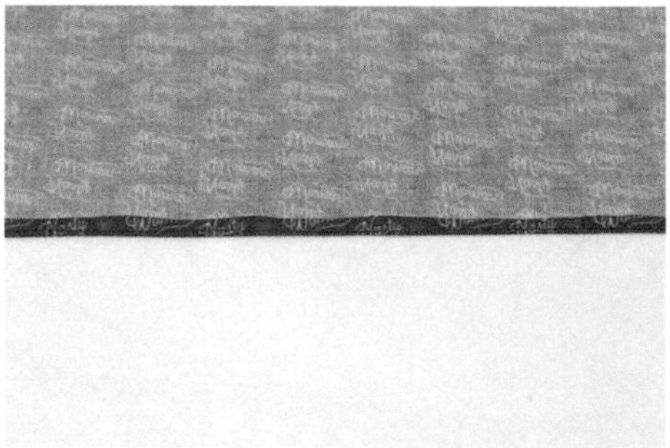

4. Miter the corners as instructed for the Quarter-Inch Hem bandanna on page 40 (see steps 3–7). If mitering these tiny corners proves too difficult, simply hem the top and bottom edges, then hem the sides. The result won't be quite as neat, but it will still look good.

Rolled Hem on a Serger

MATERIALS

1 yard of fabric

Notions

A serger that can create a rolled edge

1 cone of wooly nylon thread, to match your project

1 or 2 cones of serger thread, to match your project

Liquid seam sealant, such as Fray Check

Narrow hem worn by Megan Larson; rolled serged hem worn by Jazzmyne Johnson

CUTTING INSTRUCTIONS

Cut a piece of fabric that measures 21" x 21".

TIPS

The bulk of the previous edge can make it challenging to start a new rolled edge at the corner. I find it easier to start out by increasing the stitch length slightly and hand-cranking the machine for the first 5 stitches or so. Don't forget to turn your stitch length back to your usual setting before you take off on the rest of the edge!

INSTRUCTIONS

1. Check your serger manual and set it up for a 2-thread or 3-thread rolled edge. Use wooly nylon thread in the lower looper.
2. Serge along the top edge, using a ½-inch seam allowance.
3. Repeat on the bottom edge and each side.
4. Apply liquid seam sealant to each corner, and trim away all of the serger chain tails.

Purl-Free Pussyhats

by Lara Neel
Experience level: Beginner

> The tidings that knitters pursue their craft for reasons other than economy is not earth-shattering, for knitters have long waxed eloquent over the sensual satisfaction of rhythmically clicking needles . . . the restorative power of mindless but productive stitching when the world seems out of kilter, the freedom from guilt by putting to use the "odd moments" of one's life, the release from stress and the pleasure of participating in a chain begun long ago.
> —Anne L. Macdonald, *No Idle Hands: The Social History of American Knitting*

I don't have anything against purling, but this pattern is based on a project I use to teach my Absolute Beginner knitting students. In one fell swoop, you can avoid purling and learn to cast on, knit back and forth, knit in the round, bind off, and sew a seam. I love hats for first knitting projects because they are small, relatively easy, and giftable. If the three-needle bind off proves to be too difficult for a first-time knitter, you could always bind off in any way you prefer and sew the seam across the top of the hat. For a more experienced knitter, this hat is the perfect "mindless" knitting.

LEFT: Worn (and not worn)
by Lila Vivian Behm

MATERIALS

Yarn: Classic Elite Minnow Merino, 100% Extra Fine Superwash Merino; 77 yards/50 g skein in color, 2 skeins

Knitting needles: You should use whatever style of needles you prefer for working in the round, for a circumference two inches smaller than the desired final hat, in the size that produces a gauge you like. I used 12-inch, size 8 (5 mm) circular needles.

Notions

One stitch marker

Yarn needle

A set of double-pointed needles that are the same size as your working needles for the bind off

Ruler

Calculator or scratch paper

GAUGE

This pattern can be worked at any gauge, but you will have to create a test swatch to determine your gauge—and you want to knit it in the round. Most knitters, including me, have different gauges when they work in the round instead of working back and forth, because their purl stitches are different from their knit ones. However, working over just a few stitches, in the round, for more than a few rounds, isn't my idea of a good time. I solve this problem by making what I call a speed swatch. Use double-pointed or circular needles and cast on about 20 stitches. Knit to the end of the row. Do not turn the work. Slide the swatch back to the right end of the needle, bring the working yarn loosely around the back and knit across, again. Repeat until your gauge swatch is at least 2 inches long. The first and last stitches will look ridiculous and the back will be a mess, but you'll have a pretty good measure of your working gauge.

FINISHED MEASUREMENTS

This hat is meant to be made in any size, from baby through large adult. My example hat fits a one-year-old.

SKILLS NEEDED

You should be comfortable casting on and forming a knit stitch.

TECHNIQUE

Three-Needle Bind Off

1. Hold the right sides of the piece together on two needles.

2. Insert the third needle knitwise into the first stitch on each needle, and wrap the yarn knitwise.

3. Knit the two stitches together and slip them off the needles.
4. In the same way, knit the next two stitches together.

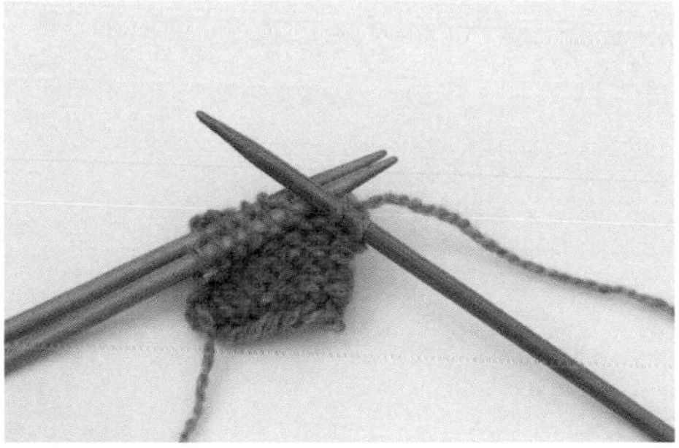

5. Slip the first stitch on the 3rd needle over the second stitch and then off the needle.

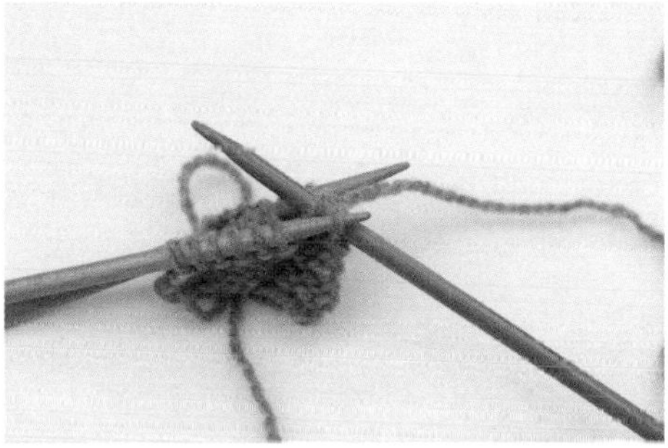

6. Repeat steps 2–5 until all stitches are bound off.

INSTRUCTIONS

1. Once you have a swatch, measure it and calculate your stitch gauge: width of swatch / number of stitches = stitch gauge (G).
2. Measure the recipient's head.
3. Remove 10% from the measurement so that your hat will fit snugly and not fall off: measurement of head x 0.9 = H.

4. Find out how many stitches to cast on by working: H x G = number of stitches to cast on.
5. Leaving a tail that is at least 6 inches long, cast on.
6. Work 8 rows back and forth in garter stitch (knitting every stitch).
7. Being careful not to twist, join your knitting to work in the round. Place a marker for the beginning of the round. Knit every stitch around to form the main body of your hat.
8. How tall (or deep) should you make your hat? It's mostly a matter of taste, but most baby hats will fit well at 5 inches deep, children's hats at 7 inches, and adult hats at 9 inches.
9. Once you have made your hat as deep as you like, divide your total number of stitches by 4 and work that many more stitches past the beginning of the round. It doesn't have to be perfectly even. This is just to move the little seam you will sew at the brim to the back of the hat.
10. Turn your hat inside out.
11. Slip half of your stitches onto one double-pointed needle and the other half onto another double-pointed needle. If they won't all fit at once, just move as many as you can, for now, and move the rest as you work.
12. Work a three-needle bind off.
13. Return to the long tail you left when you cast on and sew the two sides of the garter-stitch brim together.
14. Darn in all ends and block gently.

Worn by Lisa Neel

SEWING A FLOCK OF FLEECE PUSSYHATS

by Lara Neel

Experience Level: Beginner

I used Celia's Fleece Hat as a starting point from the Pussyhat Project.[1]

Each hat uses a strip of fleece that is 20 inches long and between 11 and 13 inches wide (I have a big noggin and I like to wear my hair in a bun, so, yes, my hat is 13 inches wide, when I cut it). The original pattern doesn't specify a seam allowance. Many people prefer to stitch thicker materials like fleece with ¼-inch seams. I used ½-inch seams, so my hats may have been smaller as a result.

If you take a 20-inch piece from 1 yard of fleece, you're left with weird scraps that are less than 16 inches long. That will work for a lot of projects, but I wanted to be able to get more Pussyhat bang for my buck. This method creates ten hats at once, in three different sizes.

MATERIALS

1¼ yards of 60-inch-wide fleece in pink

Notions

Chalk marker

Metal yardstick

Rotary cutter

Self-healing mat

Glue stick

FINISHED MEASUREMENTS

Adult Small, Medium, and Large

SKILLS NEEDED

You should be comfortable using a sewing machine.

1 "Celia's Fleece Hat," The Pussyhat Project. https://www.Pussyhatproject.com/sew/

TIPS

- If the world were perfect, I would only need a piece of fabric 40 inches long to do this, but let's face it—I'm not perfect at cutting, and neither are the helpers at the fabric store. That extra 5 inches is a little insurance for all of us. Use scraps to test machine settings or make Pussyhat bombs with them (see page 141).
- Fleece is bouncy, so cutting it is like corralling a wild animal that is made out of marshmallows. A metal yardstick, a rotary cutter, and a self-healing mat help tame the beast.
- When you're topstitching ears on hats, it can slow you down to mark where the ears should start and stop. Cut a piece of paper into the size you want and use it as a template.

INSTRUCTIONS

1. Fold your fabric in half lengthwise and place marks 6½ inches in from the fold, 12 inches from that, and 11 inches from that.

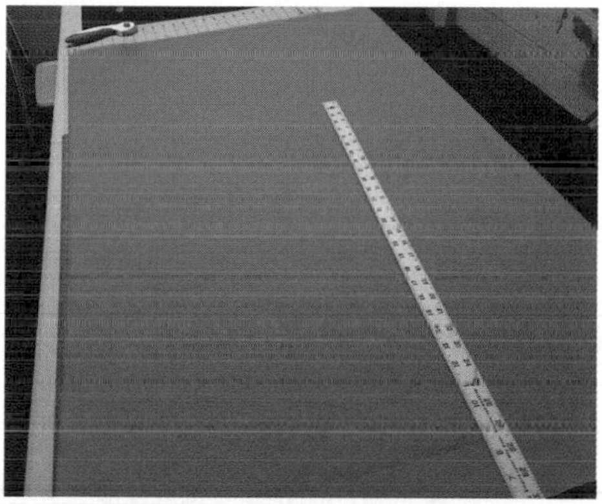

2. Using your marks as guides, cut your fabric into five long strips.

3. Unfold the strip you cut on the fold. Make sure the short end is square, trimming if needed. Cut two pieces from this strip that are each 20 inches long. Fold each piece with the right sides together, width-wise. Repeat on the other strips.

4. Stitch the sides of each hat with a ½-inch seam allowance.

5. Turn each hem up 1½ inches from the bottom and baste them in place, using the glue stick. Allow glue to dry before you proceed.

6. Using a zigzag stitch, stitch the hem in place.

7. Turn the hat right-side out. Topstitch to define each ear, starting and stopping 3 inches from the corner.

NASTY

FEM
IN
IST

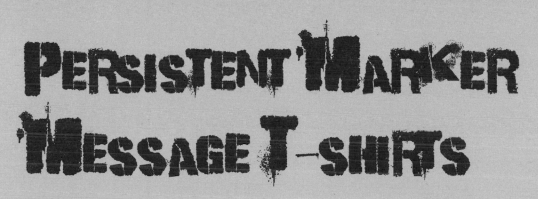

PERSISTENT MARKER MESSAGE T-SHIRTS

by Lara Neel
Experience Level: Beginner

At the best drag show I ever saw, one of the performers ripped apart their top T-shirt to reveal a scrawled message on the white tee underneath: "This Is What A Feminist Looks Like." The crowd went wild. This is a very easy, cheap, DIY way to take any message anywhere.

If the last time you ventured into the apparel arts section of the craft store was in search of puff paint, you have a pleasant surprise in your future. Permanent marker pens are now designed in a rainbow of colors and many different pen styles. They can have fine, fat, or even brush-shaped tips. Experiment to find your favorites!

MATERIALS

A purchased T-shirt

Scrap knit fabric (see tips)

A piece of cardboard that is about as wide as your shirt

Stencils (see Tips)

Ruler

Masking tape (optional)

Permanent marker pens

Notions

Scissors or a box cutter to cut cardboard

Rag for cleaning

FINISHED MEASUREMENTS

This project can be made in any size.

TIPS

- I love to use 2-inch-high alphabet stencils. The ones I use come on sheets with several letters on one sheet. I find these easier to line up than stencils where every letter is its own sheet. You may want to use smaller letters if you are creating a shirt for a child or pet.
- Choose scrap fabric that is similar to your T-shirt. I like to pick up shirts at the thrift store and use them for all kinds of projects. Often, the sleeves are just a little too short to be useful for very much. So I keep those and use them as test scraps.

INSTRUCTIONS

1. To make sure your markers don't bleed all the way through, cut a piece of cardboard so that it fits easily inside your shirt, then slip it into your shirt.

2. Cut a piece of cardboard that is about the size of a sheet of paper. You'll use this when you are cleaning your stencils.
3. Test your stencils and marking techniques on a scrap piece of fabric until you have a result you like. To get a really solid color, I like to use a very thick marker and apply it to the shirt in an up-and-down motion, as if it were a stamp. Sometimes it helps to go over the work once, leave it for a minute, then come back and go over it again.

4. As soon as you finish using any letter in your stencil set, move the stencil to your spare piece of cardboard and rub it, firmly, with your rag. This won't make it completely clean, but it helps remove excess ink.

5. I also really like the way it looks when I use a very thin marker to simply trace the outline of each letter.

6. Use a ruler to position the central letter in your motif.

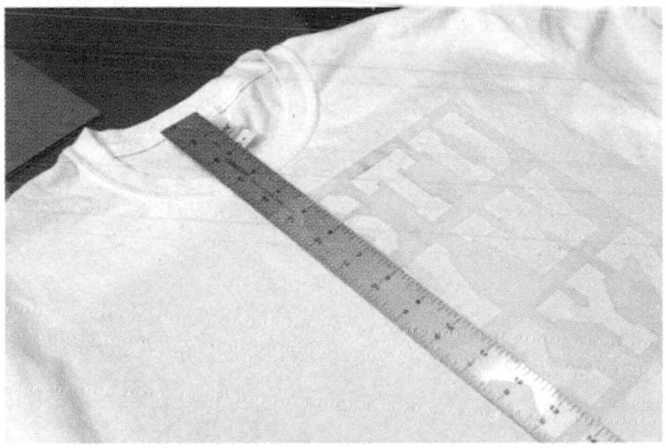

7. Add your other letters, using the central letter as a point of reference for placement. If you are worried about making your letters line up with one another, use a piece of masking tape to give yourself a straight line to place your letters against. With that said, if your second letter doesn't line up well with your first one, just throw them all out of alignment, to make it seem more intentional.

8. If you feel the alignment and spacing between your letters is very important to the success of your design, mock it up in tracing paper before you stencil your shirt.

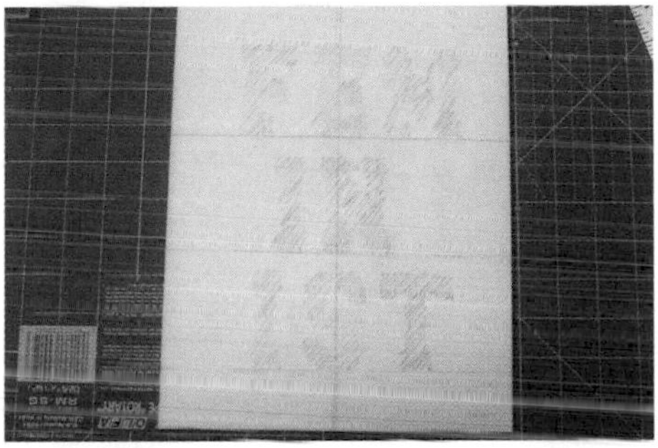

Pin your mockup in place and use that to position your letters as you work.

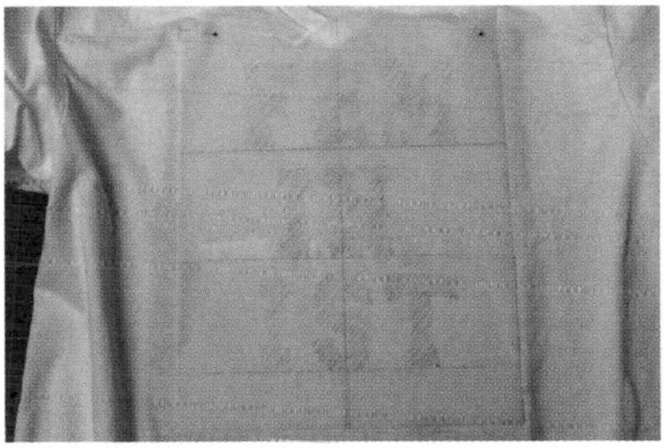

9. When you are finished, refer to the instructions that came with your pens. Some will require heat to set. Others simply need to dry for 24 hours. All will benefit from the shirt being turned inside out before washing.

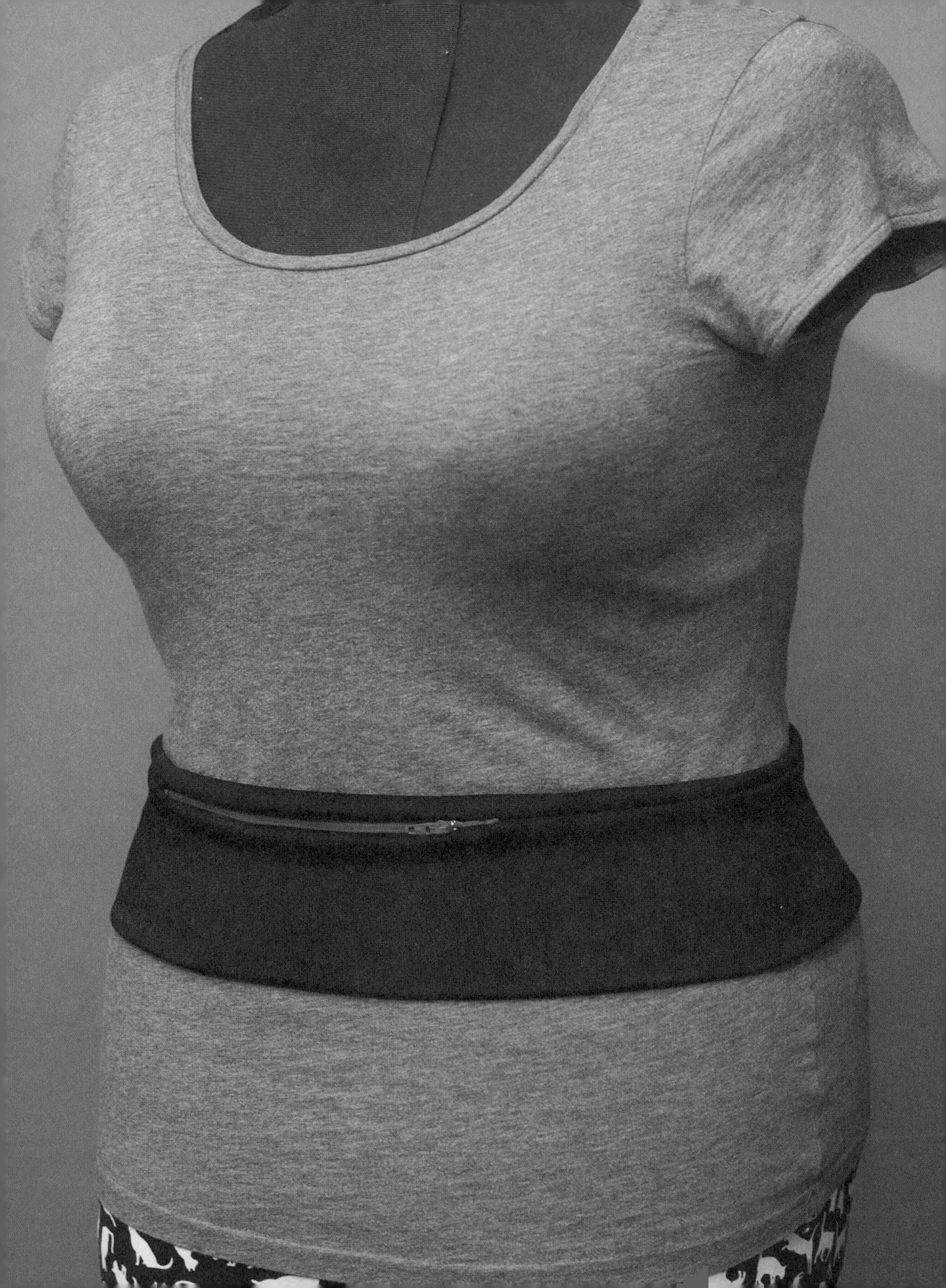

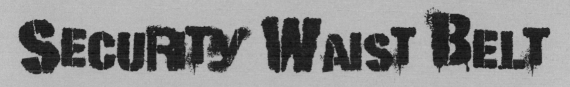

Security Waist Belt

by Lara Neel

Experience Level: Beginner

I love bags and backpacks, but sometimes you just need to have your hands completely free, and your phone and keys secure. This belt was inspired by the money belt I wear to protect my passport when I travel, but it's much more comfortable and, depending on your style, even looks pretty good over your clothes, if you want to wear it that way. Think of it as an updated, streamlined fanny pack. Or, tuck it away under your shirt and don't think about it at all.

Shrill *by Lindy West is the book to keep on your nightstand when you're preparing to protest. Lindy writes about standing up for herself, taking up space, and being loud—all important skills to have, in my opinion.*

MATERIALS

¼ yard of main fabric (see Tips)

Notions

Basic sewing kit

Matching all-purpose thread

Stretch or ball point needle

7-inch zipper

Zipper foot

Walking foot (optional)

FINISHED MEASUREMENTS

About 3.5" deep and custom-fit to the wearer.

SKILLS NEEDED

You should be comfortable using a sewing machine.

TIPS

- Choose a knit fabric that has good recovery, doesn't curl along the edges, and is fairly thick. Think pants, not a thin shirt. I've had good success with double-knit fabrics that are suggested for athletic wear. These fabrics sometimes melt if you try to press them with the iron, so test on a scrap to see how your fabric behaves.
- Sewing a stretchy fabric to a nonstretchy zipper can be a challenge, but there are ways to make it easier on yourself:
  - Use Washaway Wonder Tape to stick the two layers together. This is sold on rolls and doesn't require the heat of an iron to work.
  - Lower the presser foot pressure, if your machine has that capability.
  - Use lots of pins or clips.
  - Every few inches stop sewing, leave your needle in the fabric to hold it, and lift the presser foot to let the stretchy fabric spring back and relax.

CUTTING INSTRUCTIONS

You can make your own pattern piece for this project using paper, or simply mark and cut it on your fabric. Take the waist measurement of the person who will wear the belt and add 3 inches to it. This is the width of your pattern piece. The extra width allows for seams and also lets the belt sit a little lower on the body—about where most people would wear a regular belt.

Cut a single piece of fabric that is 8 inches tall and the width of your pattern piece. Make sure your piece is most stretchy in the direction that will wrap around the body.

INSTRUCTIONS

1. Center the zipper on one long edge of your fabric, right sides together, with the fabric on top and the zipper on bottom. Pin or baste in place (see Tips).
2. Using your zipper foot, stitch as close to the zipper's teeth as you can. Whenever you feel that the zipper pull is in your way, stop sewing with the needle down, raise the presser foot, and move it out of your way. Try to start stitching where the zipper teeth start and stop when they stop. If you stitch along the entire zipper tape, the end of the tape will show on the outside of your belt. This isn't fatal, but your work will look more polished if you can avoid it.

3. Line up the raw edge of the other long edge of your fabric, right sides together, with the other side of the zipper tape. Pin or baste in place (see Tips). Place the fabric on top and the zipper on bottom and stitch.

4. Measure the distance between the edge of the fabric and the seams you sewed for the zipper. Use this measurement as your seam allowance for the rest of the long edge. Using a standard foot or walking foot, and with your machine set to zigzag at the smallest possible width, stitch from the top of the piece to the zipper stitching. Backstitch and cut the thread. Then, stitch from the bottom of the zipper to the bottom of the piece. Try not to stitch through the sections of zipper tape at the beginning and end of the zipper. Press or carefully steam the seam allowances open so that they lie as flat as possible.

5. You will now have an inside-out tube. Unzip the zipper. Turn the bottom end of the tube to the inside and pull it as if you are going to pull the entire piece right-side out, but only bring the two raw ends even with each other, right sides together. Check to make sure that you haven't accidentally twisted your work while doing this. It's possible to make a kind of Moebius strip when finishing this piece. If that worries you, baste and check that you haven't done that before you continue.

6. Stitch the raw ends to each other, working in a circle. For small circumferences like this, I like to work from the inside of the circle, stitching slowly and rearranging my work frequently.

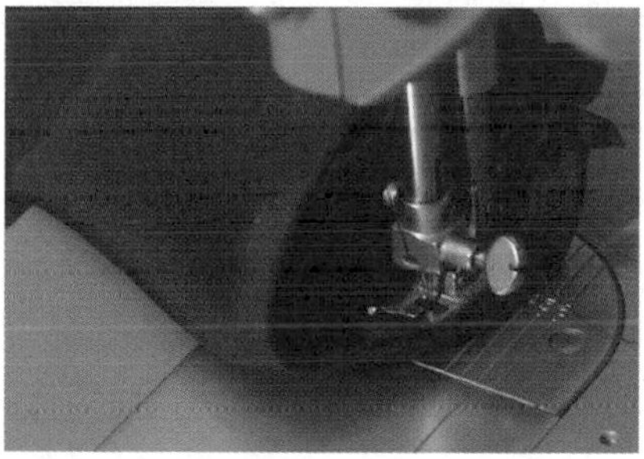

7. Turn the piece right-side out, through the zipper opening.

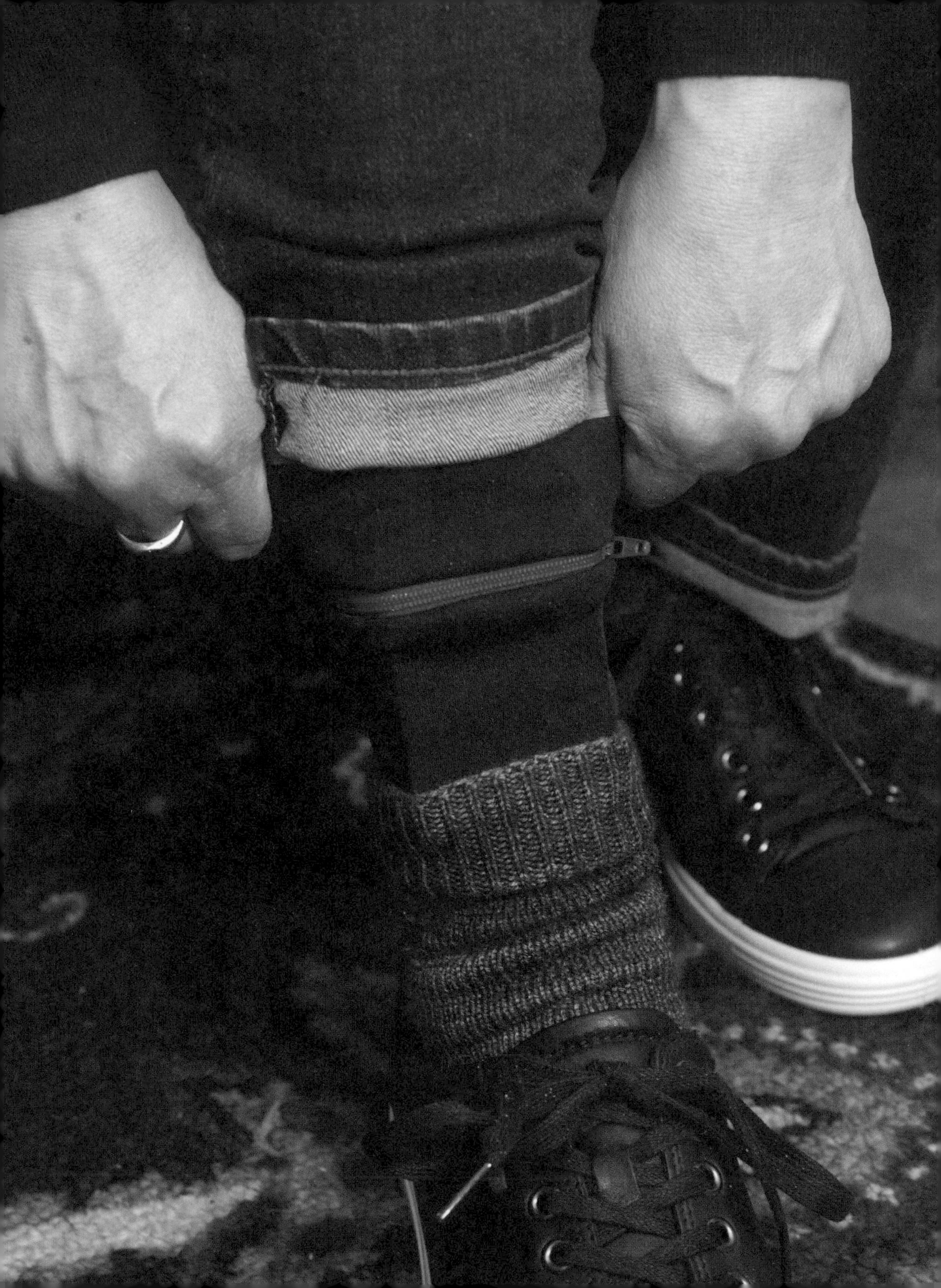

Mobility Ankle Pocket

by Lara Neel

Experience Level: Beginner

This piece works a lot like the waist belt, but can be worn around the ankle or the wrist. Unless your phone is very small, it probably won't comfortably hold that, but it can carry a little cash and a few keys.

Listen to "Free to Fight!", a self-defense project for women and compilation music album from Candy Ass Records, while you are sewing up this pattern. I had this album on a cassette tape when I was in high school. It was labeled "Scary Not Scared," and I imagine a lot of people thought that was the title for it. It was one of the first exposures I had to self-defense from a practical standpoint, and the wide range of voices on it were revelations to me.

MATERIALS

¼ yard of main fabric (see Tips)

Notions

Matching all-purpose thread

Stretch or ball point needle

7-inch zipper

Zipper foot

Walking foot (optional)

FINISHED MEASUREMENTS

About 4" deep and custom-fit to the wearer.

SKILLS NEEDED

You should be comfortable using a sewing machine.

LEFT: Worn by Dee Milroy

TIPS

Choose a knit fabric that has good recovery, doesn't curl along the edges, and is fairly thick. Think pants, not a thin shirt. I've had good success with double-knit fabrics that are suggested for athletic wear. These fabrics sometimes melt if you try to press them with the iron, so test on a scrap to see how your fabric behaves.

CUTTING INSTRUCTIONS

You can make your own pattern piece for this project using paper or simply mark and cut it on your fabric. Take the ankle measurement of the person who will wear the pocket and add 1 inch to it. This is the width of your pattern piece.

Cut a single piece of fabric that is 9 inches tall and the width of your pattern piece. Make sure your piece is most stretchy in the direction that will wrap around the body.

INSTRUCTIONS

1. Follow the instructions for the Security Waist Belt (see page 59).

Bleeding Heart T-Shirt

by Lara Neel
Experience Level: Beginner

> Most clothing is worn for social reasons—to mark sex, age, marital status, wealth, rank, modesty (whatever that may be within a particular culture), place of origin, occupation, or occasion. A few candid souls may, as the saying goes, wear their hearts on their sleeves, but we all wear a great deal of our pedigree and social aspirations written all over our apparel.
>
> —Elizabeth Wayland Barber, *Women's Work: The First 20,000 Years*

This project isn't about wearing your heart on your sleeve, but you can use it to declare your embrace of "bleeding heart" liberal ideals. I love hacking up and customizing store-bought clothing. Whenever possible, I source my to-be-altered clothing from a thrift store. I start searching among the largest T-shirts for men and work my way down the rows, looking for particular colors and fabrics. A man's size 2X shirt is often big enough for me to recut into a woman's size L T-shirt for myself. Plain black and pure white tees are the hardest to come by, in my experience. So, for this example, I purchased a black tee at a craft store. The red fabric for the heart came from a thrift-store find's sleeve.

MATERIALS

1 purchased T-shirt

⅛ yard of contrasting knit fabric

Notions

Tear-away stabilizer (I use Totally Stable by Sulky)

Matching all-purpose thread

Basic sewing kit

Applique scissors

Satin stitch or open-toe foot

Patternmaking supplies or photocopier

FINISHED MEASUREMENTS

In theory, you can complete this project using any size shirt. Shirts for children and babies might be difficult to use, though, since they are so small, unless you are willing to open up and restitch one or two seams.

CUTTING INSTRUCTIONS

For your reverse applique, cut a piece of the contrasting fabric that is large enough to cover your "bleeding heart" template (page 69), plus a few inches on every side.

TIPS

- When thrift store shopping for shirts, make sure to check the entire shirt for holes or stains. Pay extra attention to the underarms and back of the neck.
- If I get really lucky, I sometimes find sewing patterns, fabric, and notions, like zippers, at the thrift store. I grab them up immediately!
- I've had mixed results with fusible interfacings and synthetic hem tapes from thrift stores. Sometimes the fusibles don't fuse well and the tape may be too stiff to be useful. Be ready to test and throw anything out that doesn't function well.
- Sewing thread sometimes becomes weak when it ages, especially if it has been exposed to sunlight for long periods of time. Again, buyer beware. Weak thread can still be used for tasks like marking and basting, but I find it too frustrating to keep around.
- Smell everything. I know, it's weird, but some odors, like cigarette smoke, just won't ever wash out or air out. There's nothing quite like trying to work with a stinky sewing pattern.
- If your sewing machine has adjustable presser foot pressure, you may want to reduce the pressure for this project. Test on scraps, with stabilizer, until you get the results you desire.
- The stabilizer I use can be ironed on to hold it to the project, but I prefer to use pins.

Pg 69: Bleeding heart

INSTRUCTIONS

1. Trace the "bleeding heart" template (page 69) onto a tear-away stabilizer and pin it to your T-shirt, to determine where you want your motif to go. I like to do this step with the shirt right-side out. I place the motif where I want, then use pins to poke through the fabric and mark the bottom of the heart and the top of the blood drop.

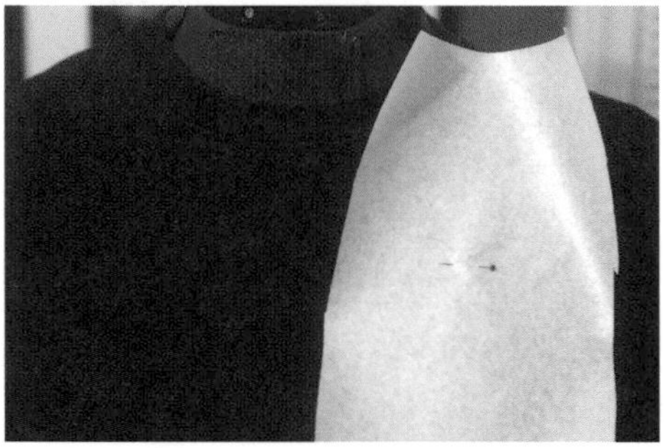

2. Turn the shirt inside out and pin the right side of the contrasting fabric to the wrong side of the shirt. Pin the stabilizer in position.

3. With the stabilizer on top, stitch around the motif, using a narrow zigzag stitch that is 20 stitches to the inch long. Work slowly. Every few inches, stop with the needle down and lift the presser foot to allow the fabric to relax.

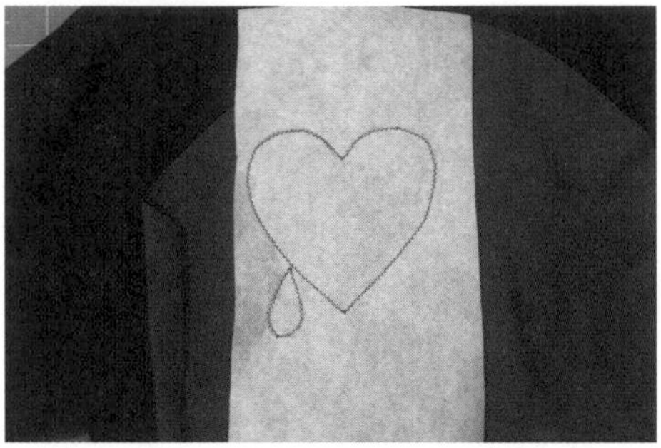

4. Gently tear away the stabilizer.

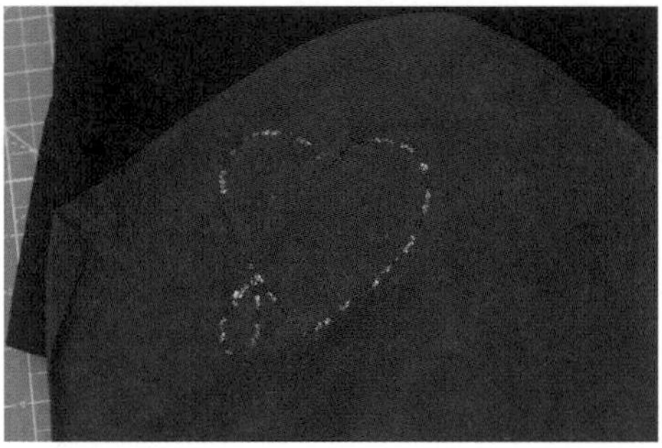

It doesn't always come away completely, but that doesn't harm the shirt.

5. Carefully trim away any excess contrasting fabric on the back of the work.

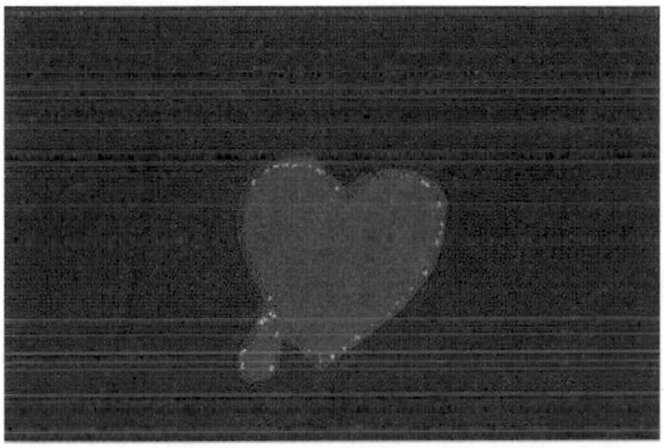

6. Turn the shirt right-side out. Using your applique scissors, carefully trim away any black fabric that is inside the stitching lines. Remember that you can always trim away more, but you can't put back something you snipped off! The black fabric on my shirt became slightly discolored while I worked. A quick trip through the washing machine sorted it out.

Snowflake Wristers

By Heather Marano
Experience Level: Intermediate

We liberals are often called "delicate snowflakes," but there isn't anything delicate about protesting. We face riotous crowds, tear gas, police presence, and many hours on our feet in all weather conditions. When you are passionate about a mission and a message, delicate does not factor into it. So I designed these wristers as a statement piece. Sure, they can be worn just to be cute or pretty, but the message is there to those who understand it.

Check out Becoming Visible *by Renate Bridenthal, Claudia Koonz, and Susan Stuard to learn more about how women used subtle messaging to advance the cause of equality in Europe's past.*

MATERIALS

Yarn: Knit Picks Wool of the Andes Superwash in Celestial (MC) and White (CC) 100% Superwash Wool 110 yards/50 g

Notions:
Needles: US size 8 (5 mm) needles, either double points, two circulars, or one long circular for magic loop

Notions:
Tapestry needle

GAUGE

22 stitches and 24 rows over 4 inches

SKILLS NEEDED

Knitting in the round, stranded colorwork.

TECHNIQUE

Two Color Cast On
With both yarns held together, make a slip knot, leaving long tails. Use the tail ends and begin long tail cast on method with one color over the thumb and the other over the index finger. To determine which color to start with, put the color that is first on the needle from the slip knot over the index finger. Whatever color is on the index finger will be the one that stays cast on to the needle.

TIPS

For knitting abbreviations, see page 175.

INSTRUCTIONS

1. Using the two color method, cast on 40 stitches. If using two circular needles, arrange 20 stitches on each needle. If using DPNs, arrange in whatever way is most comfortable for you.
2. **Ribbed cuff:** Following the colors on your needles, knit 1x1 (K1, P1) rib. My first stitch was white so in my example, the white stitches are knitted and the blue stitches are purled.
3. Knit in 1x1 rib for five rounds.
4. **Stranded colorwork section:** Knit rounds 1–21 according to the chart. Each round is repeated once so the front and the back of the wrister are identical.
5. **Ribbed cuff 2:** Just as in the beginning, knit 1x1 (K1, P1) rib for 5 rounds, using the same colors to knit or purl as you did on the first cuff.
6. Bind off in pattern. Weave in the ends.

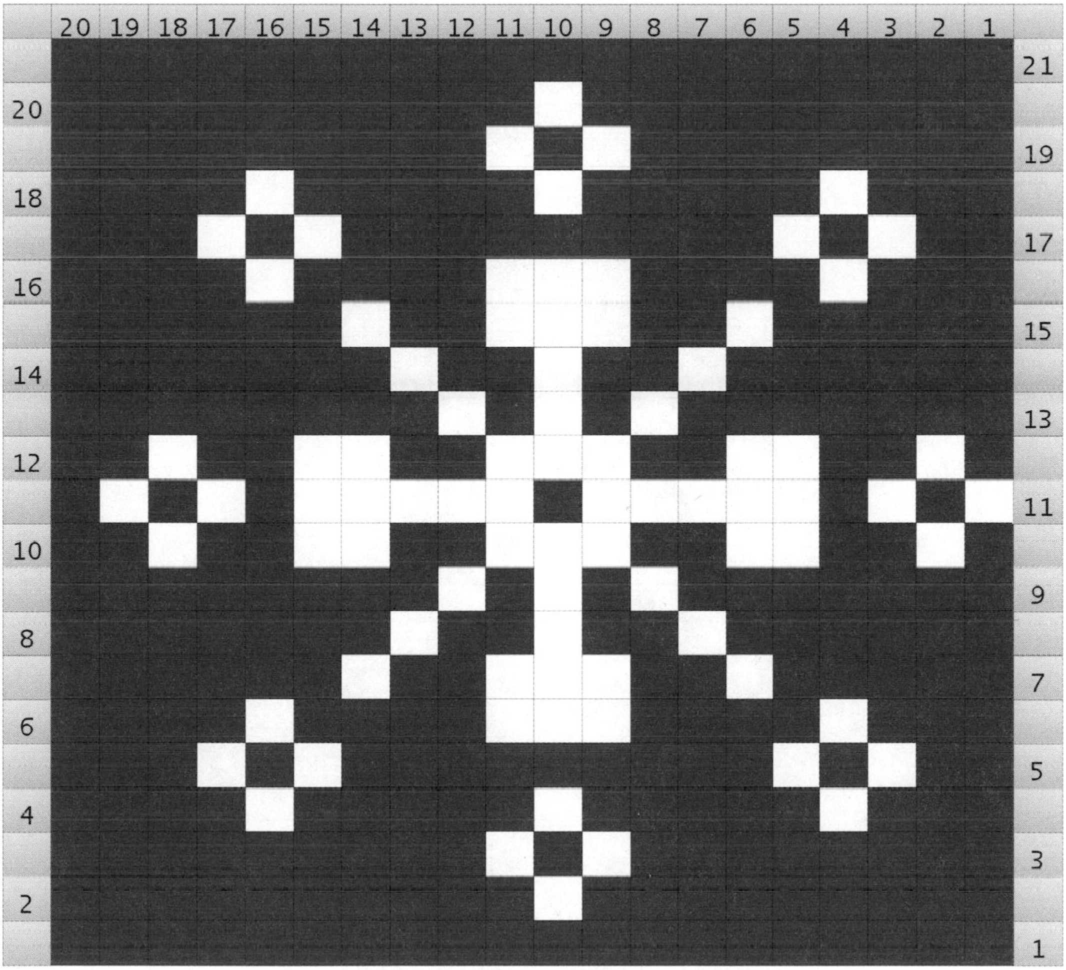
20 19 18 17 16 15 14 13 12 11 10 9 8 7 6 5 4 3 2 1
21
20
19
18
17
16
15
14
13
12
11
10
9
8
7
6
5
4
3
2
1

ck lives
atter!!

black lives
matter!!

Black Lives Matter Hat

By Donna Druchunas

Skill Level: Intermediate

I, perhaps, have a weird life and a weird family. But I prefer to think of myself as quintessentially American. I have cousins who are black, Asian, Hispanic, and white. When I was a teenager, our household included two mothers (one black and one white) and four daughters (two black and two white). We called ourselves Sisters A, B, C, and D based on our birth order. Still, as a white woman, I struggle with having white privilege and not doing all I can to oppose the systemic racism in our society. I made and wear this hat to support my sisters and cousins. Let's all work together to make a better world.

MATERIALS

Yarn: Rowan Pure Wool Worsted (219 yards/200 m per 100 g skein, 100% wool), 3 colors

- Approximately 200 yards (182 m) of black A
- 25 yards (23 m) of white B
- 10 yards (9 m) of red C

Needles: US size 7 (4.5 mm) circular needle 16 inches (40 cm) long and DPNs *or* 1 long circular needle *or* 2 short circular needles for working in the round

Notions

Tapestry needle

Stitch markers

GAUGE

20 stitches and 28 rounds = 4 inches over stockinette stitch

FINISHED MEASUREMENTS

20"-long circumference, will stretch to fit adult head several inches larger

SKILLS NEEDED

Knit, purl, knitting in the round, stranded colorwork.

TECHNIQUE

Seed Stitch

1. Round 1: (K1, P1) around
2. Round 2: (P1, K1) around
3. Repeat rounds 1 and 2 for pattern

TIPS

For knitting abbreviations, see page 175.

INSTRUCTIONS

1. With A, CO 96 stitches. Join to knit in the round.

Brim:

2. Work in seed stitch for 1 inch or desired length for brim.

Body:

3. Change to stockinette stitch.
4. Knit 2 rounds, and increase with kfb to 97 stitches.
5. Set up chart: With A and B, work stitches 1–57 once, then work 2-st repeat of sts 58 and 59 to end of round. After completing all rows of chart with A and B, change back to A and knit 2 rounds or until hat measures approximately 6 inches from CO edge, or 3¼ inches less than desired length.

Crown

6. Next round: Knit to last 2 stitches, k2tog—96 stitches.
7. Next round: (K12, pm) around—8 sections of 12 stitches.
8. Decrease round: (Knit to last 2 stitches before marker, k2tog) around.
9. Next round: Knit all stitches.
10. Repeat last 2 rounds until 8 stitches remain; switching to double points when necessary.

Finishing:

11. Cut yarn, leaving a 4-inch-long tail. Run the tail through the remaining stitches and gently tug to fasten off and gather in top of hat. Put the tail to the inside of the hat.
12. Weave in ends. Wash and dry flat to block.

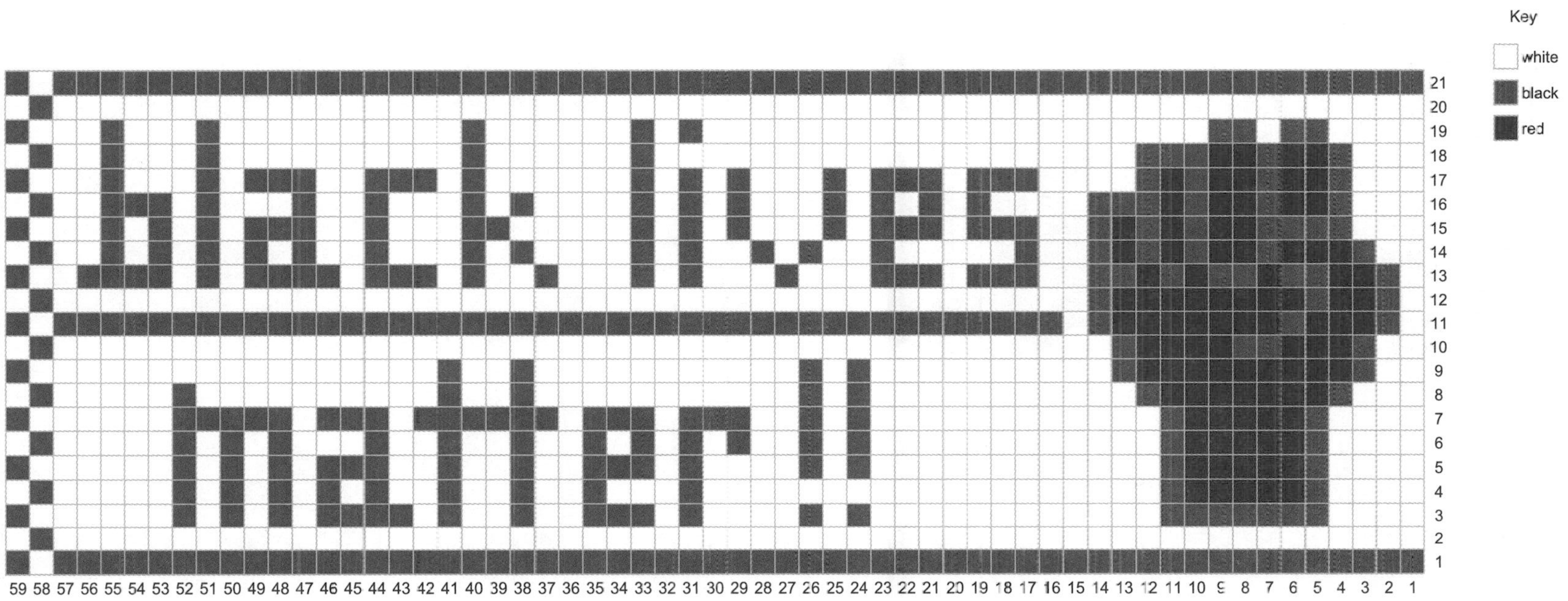
Key
white
black
red
black lives
matter!!

I raise up my voice—not so I can shout but so that those without a voice can be heard . . . we cannot succeed when half of us are held back.

—Malala Yousafzai

At Home

Pussyhat Throw Pillow

by Lara Neel
Experience Level: Beginner

> Creation from chaos is natural. We've come to a place here we've realized that we have this actual, physical need to create things . . . we're sick of homogenized culture, and these realizations have left holes in our hearts. We create to fill those holes, to be able to sleep at night knowing we've done something, even a small something, to confront the manufactured culture that is currently being churned out.
>
> —from the Antifesto in *AntiCraft: Knitting, Beading and Stitching for the Slightly Sinister* by Renee Rigdon and Zabet Stewart

If looking like you're wearing a Pussyhat when you take a nap on the couch appeals to you, you might want to check out The Bitch in the House *by Cathi Hanauer.*

MATERIALS

1 yard of pink fleece

14-inch round pillow form

Notions

Matching all-purpose thread

Basic sewing kit

Walking foot

Fabric glue stick

String

2 pencils

Patternmaking supplies

FINISHED MEASUREMENTS

14" around, plus ears

BOTTOM: With Sabine Behm

TIPS

Please read the tips for the Pussyhat Pet Bed on pages 88 and 89.

With Lila Vivian Behm

MAKE PAPER PATTERNS

Make a paper pattern for the front of the cushion (full circle):

Use paper that is at least 15 inches across in both directions, or tape paper together until it is large enough. Tie a loop in the end of your string so that it fits around a pencil but can still turn freely. Tie another loop, 7½ inches away from the first loop, for a second pencil. Hold one pencil near the center of your paper and use the other to draw a circle.

Cut out your circle. Fold it in half to crease it. This crease is your grainline. Along the outside edge, measure 1¼ inches to the right of the grain line, and place a mark. Repeat, 1¼ inches to the left of the grainline. These two marks are what you will use to align the "ears."

Make a paper pattern for the back pieces:

Use a piece of paper that is at least 15 inches across and 10½ inches long. Fold 1 inch down across the long side so that your piece is now 15 inches wide and 9½ inches long. Place the center of your full circle piece 2 inches below the top of your paper, with the grainline perpendicular to the folded edge. Cut away all of the paper that is not covered. Unfold the piece when you are finished.

CUTTING INSTRUCTIONS

From fleece: Using the patterns, cut 1 front piece (full circle), 2 back pieces, and 4 ears (page 91).

INSTRUCTIONS

1. Baste the straight edges of your back pieces, using glue stick, with a 1-inch hem. Set aside to dry.

2. Place the ears' right sides together. With a straight stitch, stitch around the left and right sides of the ear, leaving the bottom open. Repeat on the other ear.

3. Trim away the top corners of the ears, taking care not to cut through the stitching.

4. Turn the ears right-side out and trim the seam allowance at the bottom corners.

5. Align the inner corners of the ears with the notches on the front of your pillow and baste them in place, right sides together.

6. With a ⅝-inch seam and a zigzag stitch, stitch the hems on the back pieces.

7. Stack your pieces. Place your front piece right-side up, the upper back piece wrong-side up and the lower back piece wrong-side up.

8. With a straight stitch, stitch all the way around, with a ½-inch seam allowance. Backstitch at the beginning and end of this seam.

9. Turn right-side out, and insert the pillow form.

PUSSYHAT PET BED

by Lara Neel

Experience Level: Beginner

I wanted to make a pet bed, and I couldn't resist the idea of making one in the Pussyhat image. This is really very simple to make, once you get the hang of working with fleece. I made my own cushion to put inside it, so that the fleece cover can be washed. A few years ago, I foolishly skipped this step and simply stuffed a fleece cat bed. I ended up having to throw it out after it became completely covered in cat fur! The cushion has a zipper, so you can adjust the level of stuffing according to your pet's desires. I had to come up with a way to give the ears some body, yet still be sure they wouldn't just bunch up or flatten out when washed. I'm very happy with my results.

MATERIALS

1½ yards of pink fleece

1 yard of insert fabric (see Tips)

Notions

Matching all-purpose thread

Basic sewing kit

18- to 20-inch zipper

Stuffing (see Tips)

Walking foot

Zipper foot

Fabric glue stick

Washaway Wonder Tape

String

2 pencils

Patternmaking supplies

FINISHED MEASUREMENTS

24" around, plus ears

TOP LEFT and BOTTOM LEFT: With Travis

TIPS

- I knew the fleece would hide any fabric I put underneath it, so I used an old bedsheet to make my insert.
- If this is your first zipper, don't sweat it. The zipper will be hidden inside your pet bed, so if it's not beautiful, it won't matter in the least.
- I had the best results when I cut the full circle from the edge of the fabric, then used the rest of the width along that part of my material to cut the back pieces. Don't forget to mark the notches on your full circle pattern piece with a small snip in the fleece.
- When you are cutting out your ears, don't forget to cut mirror images half of the time. You can take care of this either by cutting through two layers that are back-to-back or by flipping the pattern pieces over.
- I like to stack the ears, wrong sides together, as I cut them, so that I know I have enough of each side.
- Many people suggest that fleece should always be cut with the nap all running the same direction. This may or may not matter to you. In any case, the inner ears will be invisible when the work is finished, so feel free to cut them any way you like, as long as the grainline is correct.
- You could use fiberfill for stuffing, but my favorite method is also a scrap-buster. I keep a basket under my cutting table. Whenever I have scraps from a project, I set aside what I need to test machine settings. Then, I use my rotary cutter and slice everything else into 2-inch-wide strips. I throw those into my basket. When the basket is full, I make a pet bed. Fleece scraps are light and lofty. Knit scraps have a nice heft to them. Even woven scraps work as stuffing, but lend a firmer feel to the piece.
- I like the way a wide zigzag stitch looks on fleece, but sometimes this can cause stitches to skip. Test your settings until you are happy with your results.

- If you have trouble placing the thick fleece under your presser foot, use a thin plastic tool, like the tools used to thread drawstrings through casings, to help things along. Don't stitch over the tool, just use it to position the fleece under your presser foot.

- Double-check to make sure your presser foot is down before you begin sewing. It can be hard to see that your foot is in the up position when you are using thicker fabrics.
- Fleece can shed quite a bit and that's rather hard on sewing machines. Take the time to clean your machine after you finish this project, even if you don't do that as a matter of course.

MAKE PAPER PATTERNS

Make a paper pattern for the front of the pet bed and the insert (full circle):

Use paper that is at least 25 inches across in both directions or tape paper together until it is large enough. Tie a loop in the end of your string so that it fits around a pencil, but can still turn freely. Tie another loop, 12½ inches away from the first loop, for a second pencil. If your measurement isn't exact, your pet bed will simply be slightly larger or smaller than the sample. Hold one pencil near the center of your paper and use the other pencil to draw a circle.

Cut out your circle. Fold it in half to crease it. This crease is your grainline. Along the outside edge, measure 3¼ inches to the right of the grainline, and place a mark. Repeat this 3¼ inches to the left of the grainline. These two marks are what you will use to align the "ears."

Make a paper pattern for the back pieces:

Use a piece of paper that is at least 25 inches across and 15½ inches long. Fold 1 inch down across the long side, so that your piece is now 25 inches wide and 14½ inches long. Place the center of your front pet bed pattern piece 2 inches below the top of your paper, with the grainline perpendicular to the folded edge. Cut away all of the paper that is not covered by your front pet bed pattern piece. Unfold the piece when you are finished.

Assemble the outer ear pattern piece: Copy or trace each piece, cut them out, and use the registration marks to align them. Make sure that the round mark matches up to the round mark and the square mark to the square mark.

CUTTING INSTRUCTIONS

From fleece: Cut 1 front piece (full circle), 2 back pieces, 4 outer ears (page 92), and 4 inner ears (page 91).

From insert fabric: Cut 2 insert pieces (full circles).

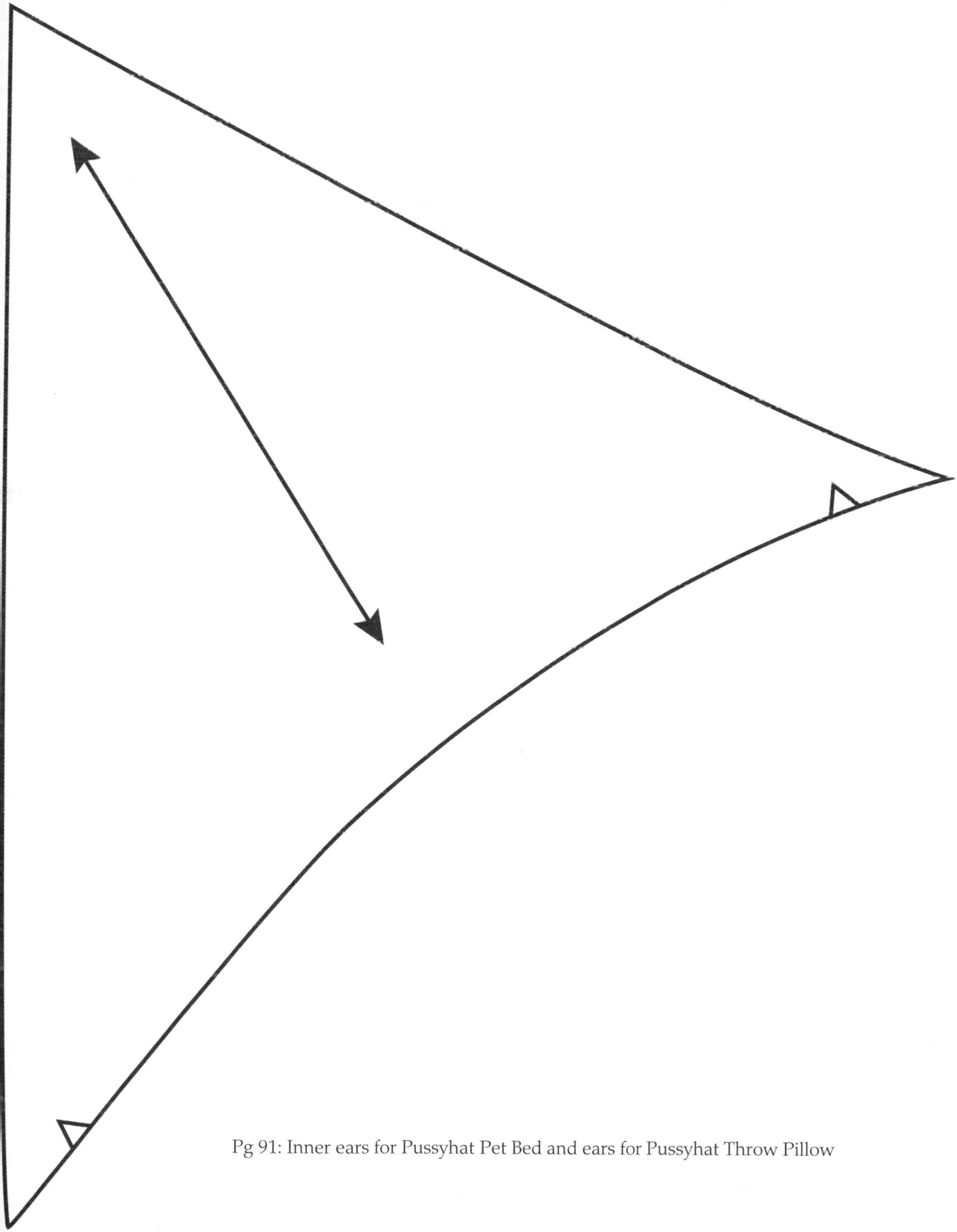

Pg 91: Inner ears for Pussyhat Pet Bed and ears for Pussyhat Throw Pillow

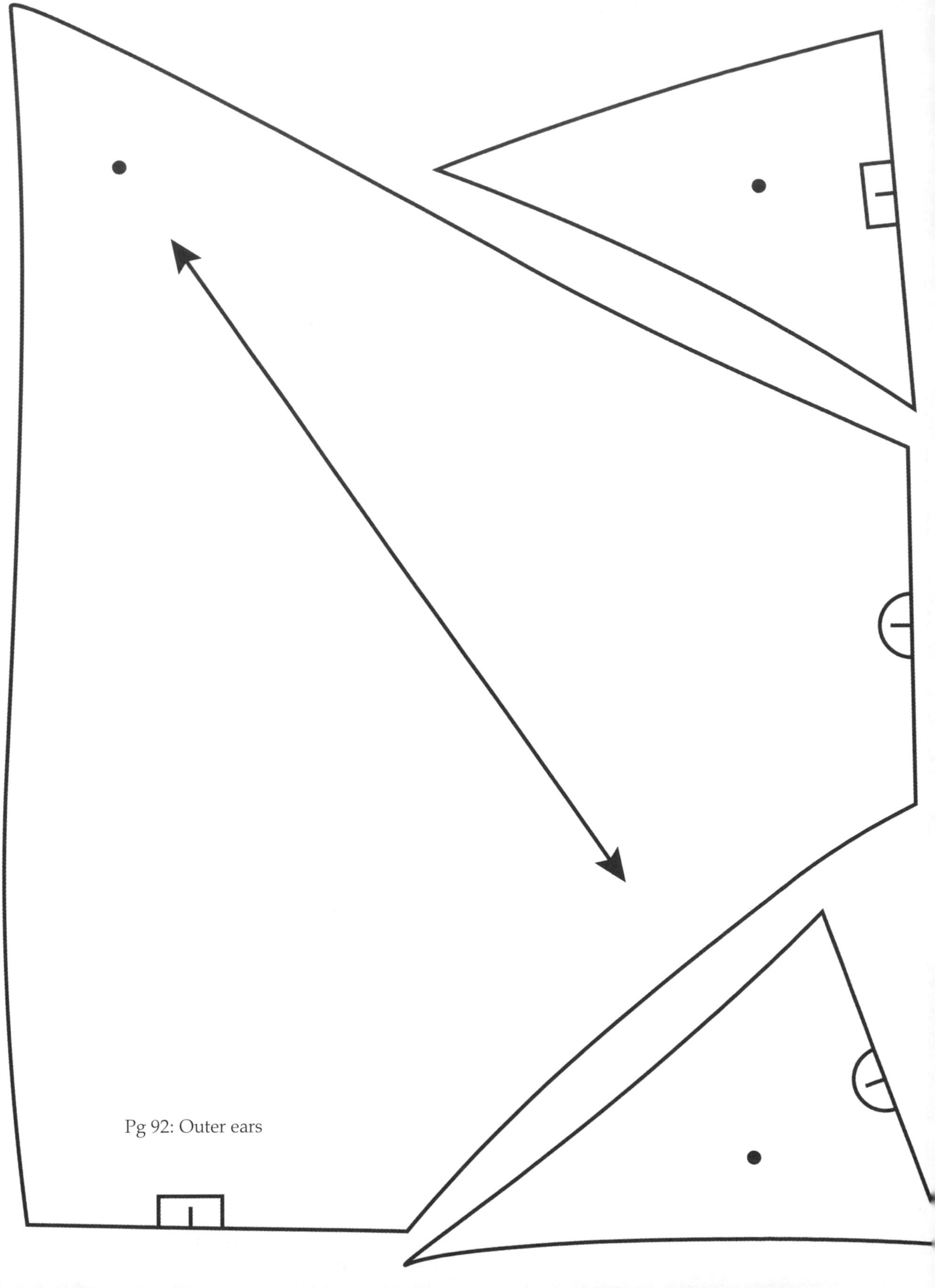
Pg 92: Outer ears

INSTRUCTIONS

1. Baste the straight edges of your back pieces using a glue stick, with a 1-inch hem. Set aside to dry.

2. Lay out one of your insert pieces. Lay your zipper along one edge of the piece. Place marks for where the zipper begins and ends. Set the zipper aside.

3. Using the longest stitch setting on your machine, stitch the two sides of the insert to each other, with a ½-inch seam allowance, from the top of your zipper mark to the bottom of your zipper mark. Using a regular stitch length, stitch for a few inches on either side of this section, backstitching at the beginning and end of these short seams. Press these seams open.

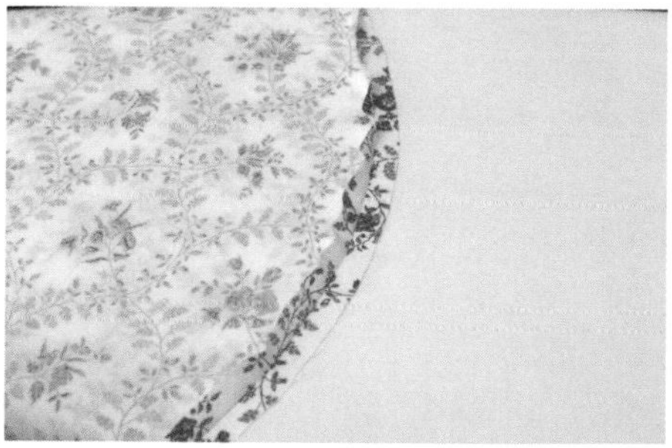

4. Using Washaway Wonder Tape, attach the zipper to the basted section of your insert.

5. Switch to a zipper foot. Stitch all around the zipper, close to the zipper teeth, through all layers. This is a curved edge, but it's a very gentle curve, so work slowly and it should be easy to do.

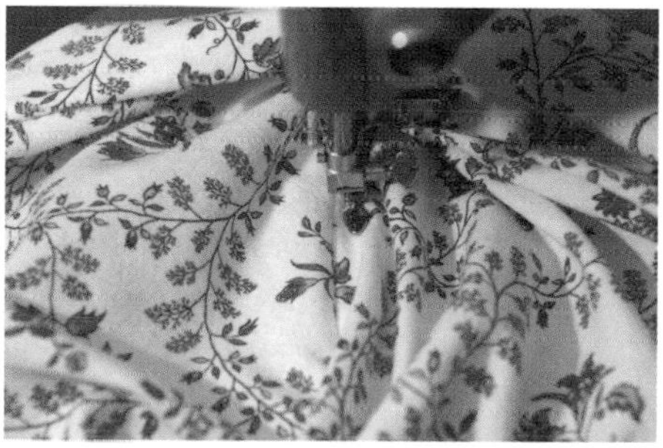

6. Remove the basting stitches to reveal your zipper. Use a seam ripper, if needed.

7. Turn your insert insideout and unzip it. Using either your all-purpose foot or a walking foot, stitch the rest of the way around the insert. Backstitch at the beginning and end of this seam to secure it.

8. Turn your insert right-side out and stuff it.

9. Switch to your walking foot. Place your inner ears wrong sides together and stitch around them, using a zigzag stitch and a ¼-inch seam allowance.

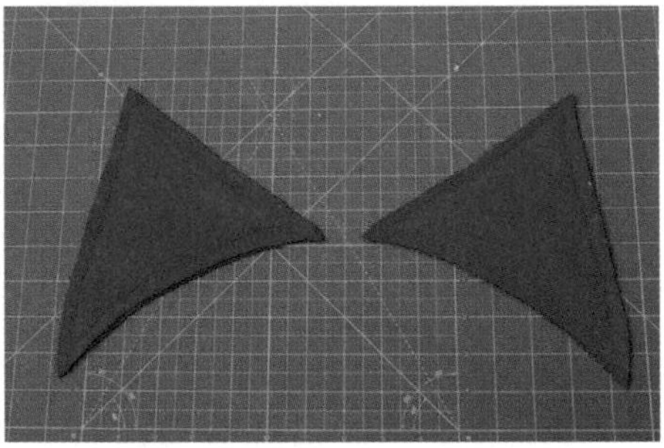

10. Using the placement dots on your pattern piece, stitch 1 inner ear to an outer ear, with the right side of the inner ear to the wrong side of the outer ear. Repeat on the other ear, making sure that the pieces you are using are mirror images of the first ear.

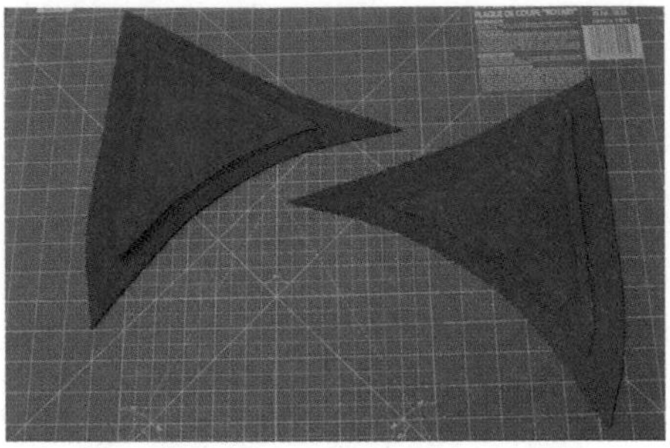

11. Place the second piece for the outer ear against the one you just stitched, right sides together. With a straight stitch, stitch around the left and right sides of the ear, leaving the bottom open. Repeat on the other ear, making sure that the pieces you are using are mirror images of the first ear.

12. Trim away the top corners of the outer ears, taking care not to cut through the stitching.

13. Turn the ears right-side out and trim the seam allowance at the bottom corners.

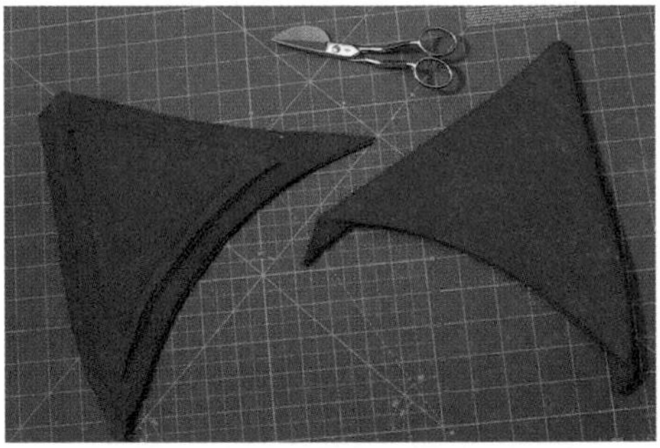

14. Align the inner corners of the ears with the notches on the front of your pet bed and baste them in place, right sides together.

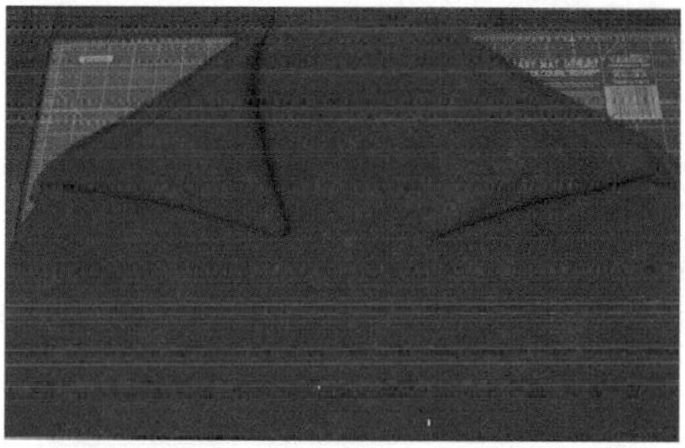

15. With a ⅝-inch seam and a zigzag stitch, stitch the hems on the back pieces.

16. Stack your pieces. Place your front piece right-side up, the upper back piece wrong-side up, and the lower back piece wrong-side up.

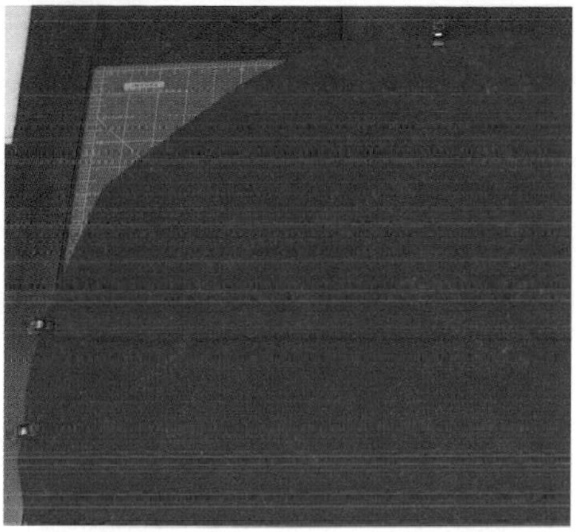

17. With a straight stitch, stitch all the way around the bed, using a ½-inch seam allowance. Backstitch at the beginning and end of this seam.

18. Turn right-side out and fill with the insert.

Luscious Lounge Slippers

By Heather Marano

Experience Level: Beginner

Rest your weary feet in these fluffy lounge slippers. They are easy to knit up and have that retro '50s vibe. Play with color with these. Want baby pink slippers with sexy black roses and trim? Go for it! Self-care is just as important as maintaining the resistance. In fact, it's vital to prevent burnout. So, grab that mug of tea, curl up in your favorite chair with your favorite book, and keep your feet toasty warm in these lovely slippers.

While you are at it, check out SARK's great book Succulent Wild Woman *and nourish your body and soul.*

MATERIALS

Yarn for slippers:

> 1 skein Cascade 128 Superwash Merino Wool in White (MC); 100 g/3.5 oz, 128 yards/117 m
>
> 1 skein Cascade 128 Superwash Merino Wool in Ruby (CC); 100 g / 3.5 oz, 128 yards/117 m

Knitting needles: One pair US size 10.5 (6.5 mm) needles and an additional US size 10.5 needle for the three-needle bind off (or sizes needed to obtain gauge)

Notions

Tapestry needle

US K (6.5 mm) crochet hook

4 stitch markers

GAUGE

14 stitches over 4 inches, 16 rows per 4 inches.

FINISHED MEASUREMENTS

Approximately 9" x 4" for a size 9 shoe. Adjust length of initial garter stitch section for each change in shoe size.

For example, for a size 7 shoe, knit garter stitch for 4 inches instead of 6 inches as for the size 9 shoe.

SKILLS NEEDED

Garter stitch, basic decreases, three-needle bind off, crochet.

TECHNIQUE

Three-Needle Bind Off
(See page 47 for instructions.)

TIPS

For knitting abbreviations, see page 175.

INSTRUCTIONS

Slipper (make two)

1. Using the long tail cast on method, CO 32 stitches with your main color.
2. Knit each row (garter stitch) until the piece measures 6 inches from cast on edge.

Increase rows

3. Next row: K1, kfb, knit until you have two stitches on the right needle, kfb, K1—34 stitches.
4. Repeat increase row one more time—36 total stitches.
5. Knit in garter stitch for 1 inch. Place a marker here to keep track of how far to sew the toe seam.

Increase rows

6. Next Row: K1, kfb, knit until you have two stitches on the right needle, kfb, K1—38 stitches.
7. Repeat increase row one more time—40 stitches.

Set up row

8. K9, pm, K2, pm, K18, pm, K2, pm, K

Shape toe

9. Next row: K5, ssk, K2, sm, K2, sm, K2tog, knit to two stitches before the marker, ssk, sm, K2, sm, K2, K2tog, K5—36 stitches
10. Next row: knit all stitches.
11. Next row: K5, ssk, K1, sm, K2, sm, K2tog, knit to two stitches before the marker, ssk, sm, K2, sm, K1, K2tog, K5—32 stitches
12. Next row: knit all stitches.
13. Next row: K5, ssk, sm, K2, sm, K2tog, knit to two stitches before the marker, ssk, sm, K2, sm, K2tog, K5—28 stitches.
14. Next row: knit all stitches.
15. Turn and knit first 14 stitches of row, then cut the yarn, leaving a

long tail. Place last 14 stitches of row on same needle as first 14 stitches. Using the three-needle bind off, join these 28 stitches to close the toe. Sew the center seam from the toe to the marker. Sew the back heel seam. Weave in any ends.

Crochet Flower (make two)

16. (RS): with crochet hook and contrasting color yarn, ch 32, tr in fifth ch from the hook, (2 tr in next ch) nine times, (2 dc in next ch) twelve times, (2 hdc in next ch) seven times. Bind off leaving a 6-inch tail.

17. Starting with the hdc end, roll the piece into a flower and use the tail to sew it together and then to the slipper on the top of the toe. Weave in the end.

Needle Felted Wool Coasters

By Heather Marano

Experience Level: Beginner

Felted wool is one of the oldest fiber treatments in the world. Prior to the spinning of wool to make yarn or thread, it's believed felting was the main method of wool production for fabric creation. Many cultures have myths surrounding the origins of feltmaking. Among the ancient Sumerians, the discovery of felting was attributed to Urnamman, a famous Sumerian war hero. In the story of Saint Clement and Saint Christopher, we are told that men fleeing persecution stuffed wool into their sandals to protect their feet. At the end of their journey, all the movement, sweat, and heat created felt. The oldest archeological evidence for felting hails from Turkey. Wall paintings dating back 5,000 to 8,500 years ago show evidence of felt applique. A tomb in Southern Siberia containing felted fiber was found with a nomadic tribal elder dating 7,000 years ago. And we are still felting wool today. Sometimes not by choice. We all know the feeling when we pull our favorite wool sweater from the dryer and see that it will now only fit the cat.

These coasters are felted wool done not with heat and water, but with felting needles. It's an easy project that anyone can do. Get creative with your motifs. If gender symbols aren't your bag, opt for something more complex, like a snowflake or a raised fist. The possibilities are endless.

MATERIALS

2 oz raw, clean, unspun wool

4 yards of yarn in the colors of your choice: I chose red for this project

Notions

Felting needle

Felting pad

FINISHED MEASUREMENTS

3.5" in diameter, but you can make these as big as you like.

TIPS

- The coarser your wool, the better. You can purchase roving for this project, or you can purchase smaller amounts of raw wool from a seller on Etsy. There are many shepherdesses who sell their sheared wool on Etsy and it's a great way to support a small business, and get your hands on some beautiful, fluffy, unprocessed wool.
- You can purchase felting needles and felting pads at most craft stores. The needle is designed with tiny backward-facing barbs so that each time it is pushed in and out of the wool, it compacts and felts it. The pad is what you felt on so that you don't damage the needle or the surface under the pad.
- WARNING! Felting needles are *extremely* sharp and can do serious damage to fingers and hands. This is not a project for doing in front of the TV. Absolute attention is required. You can find little leather finger guards to wear to help protect you from an accidental stab.

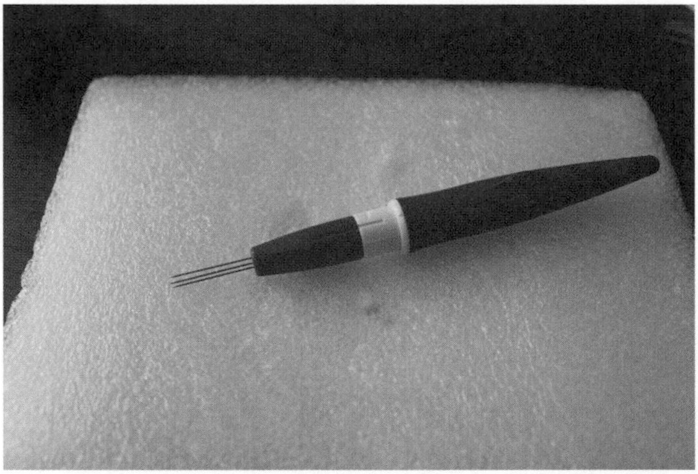

INSTRUCTIONS

1. Gather a handful of your wool (I take about ¼ oz) and shape it to the approximate size you want the coaster to be. Place this on the felting mat.

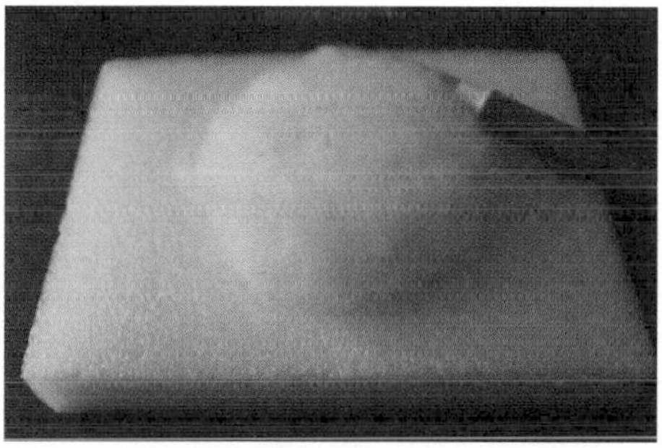

2. Using your felting needle, begin to lightly punch the needle through the wool and into the mat. You don't need to be aggressive with this; a light touch will save your needles and your mat, and still get the job done.

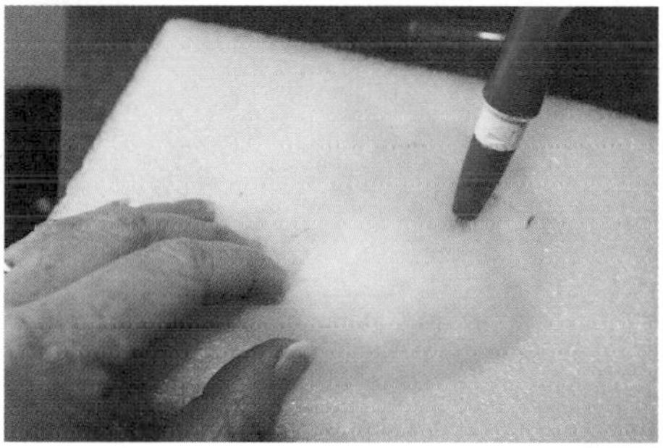

3. Continue in this fashion until the wool has been flattened equally around the piece. Gently peel the wool from the mat, flip it over, and repeat step 2. Once your wool is as felted as you'd like it to be, it's time to add your embellishments.

4. Using your felting needle and your chosen yarn, *very carefully* attach the yarn to the edge of the coaster with your felting needle. You will need to go over this edging a few times to ensure a good attachment. Then use your yarn to add whatever symbols or messages you want on the inside of the circle.

LOVE IS LOVE IS LOVE IS LOVE IS

QUILTED MUG RUG

by Lara Neel

Experience Level: Beginner

> I was determined to create a world for myself where my creativity could be respected and sustained. It is a world still in the making . . . Women artists cannot wait for ideal circumstances to be in place before we find the time to do the work we are called to do; we have to create oppositionally, work against the grain.
>
> —bell hooks, *Art on My Mind*

I thought about this quote a great deal as I was working on this book. So much in life just isn't possible until you can say, "I need this space for my work," or, "I scheduled this time to sew."

A mug rug is larger than a coaster, but smaller than a placemat. I like them because they are small, fun to make, and make me feel like less of a slob when I just want somewhere to put my spoon. A mug rug could also function as a daily reminder to yourself, or a friend, that even just a small space, set aside, can make a difference in your ability to take care of yourself. Quilting purists may object to my use of polyester fleece instead of batting. I chose it because it's inexpensive, it won't bunch up like some other types of batting, and, if you're making other projects in this book, you probably already have a little piece of it in your stash box.

MATERIALS

¼ yard of main fabric

¼ yard of polyester fleece

¼ yard of lining fabric

Notions

Matching all-purpose thread

Basic sewing kit

Ball point sewing machine needle (see Tips)

Chalk marker (see Tips)

Walking foot

Ruler

Self-healing mat

Washaway Wonder Tape

FINISHED MEASUREMENTS

4" x 6"

TIPS

- The fleece is sandwiched in between your main fabric and your lining fabric, so the color doesn't matter very much, but some colors will show through fabrics with light backgrounds. White is probably the safest bet unless your fabrics have black backgrounds. Then, choose black fleece. Whenever you stop by the fabric store, check out the remnant bins. You can often find fleece there in just about any color.
- Fleece will melt if you press it with a hot iron, so be careful! When in doubt, test on a scrap. I like to hover the iron over the piece, hit it with a puff of steam, and flatten it with a tailor's clapper.
- This project combines woven fabric with fleece, which is a knit. Test several needles until you find one that works well with this combination and doesn't cause your stitches to skip. I ended up using a size 100/16 ball point needle.
- I find that white chalk markers are the easiest to remove from fabric. Marking white chalk on mostly-white fabric may seem a little crazy, but it's easier to see than you would think. If this really drives you nuts, try your favorite method of marking, but make sure it will come out of the fabric when you are finished.
- The Resist Pussyhat Pussycat print I used for this project was designed by Donna Druchunas. If you'd like to use it, you can purchase it on Spoonflower.com. I chose their Basic Cotton Ultra base.

CUTTING INSTRUCTIONS

Cut one 4.5" x 6.5" piece from main fabric.

Cut one 4.5" x 6.5" piece from polyester fleece (see Tips).

Cut one 4.5" x 6.5" piece from lining fabric.

INSTRUCTIONS

1. Lay main fabric on the self-healing mat at a 45-degree angle. Using chalk marker and ruler, mark lines 1 inch apart from each other, across the piece.

2. Baste fleece to the main fabric, wrong sides together, as close to the edge as you can.
3. Stitch across each of the marked lines.

4. Place lining fabric over the quilted piece, right sides together. Place marks 2 inches from each side along one of the long edges. With a ¼-inch seam allowance, stitch around the piece, leaving the section between the marks open.

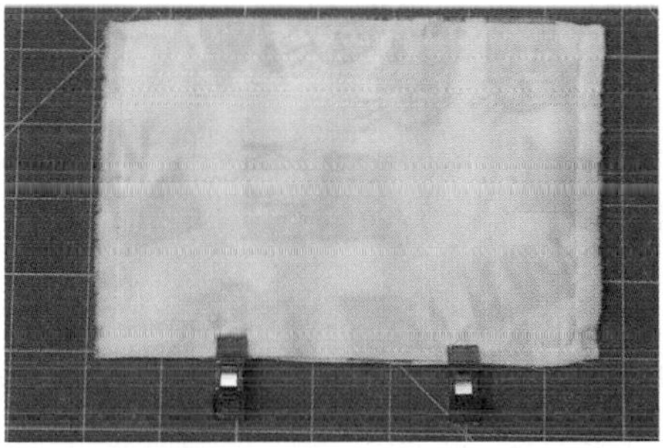

5. Trim away the seam allowance from each of the corners.

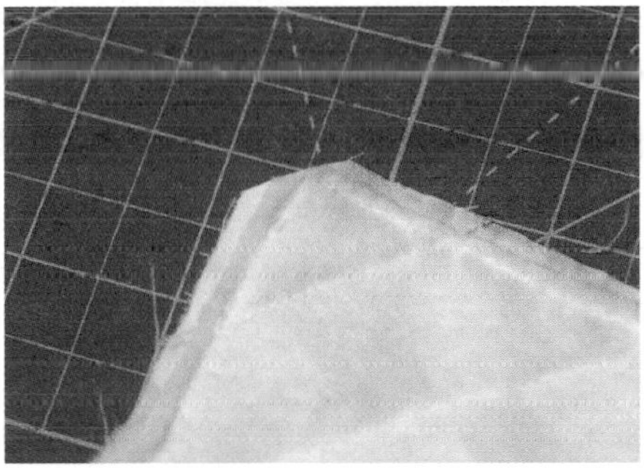

6. Turn the piece right-side out, through the open section. Press carefully (see Tips).
7. Use a little Washaway Wonder Tape to keep the open section in place. Topstitch as close to the edge as you can, all the way around. When you start and stop topstitching, don't backstitch. Just set stitch length to 0 and take 2 or 3 stitches to secure your line of stitching.

Resist!

Well Read Bookmarks

By Heather Marano

Experience Level: Advanced

I am a voracious reader. In 2016, I had a goal to read sixty books and read eighty-five. My goal for 2017 is a hundred, and as of the end of April I'm already thirty in. When I am out walking, in my favorite chair knitting, cooking dinner, or folding laundry, I listen to audiobooks. But at night, I read physical books in bed. I just love the feel and smell of real books. Yes, I have a tablet, and I read books to my boys at night from it, but I really enjoy the feel of a book in my hand. If you read physical books, you need good bookmarks. I often have two or three books going at once, so I employ a number of bookmarks at the same time.

This one is not only a reminder of the message, but it's also super fun to knit. It's done with the double knitting method so the back is a mirror image of the front and all the stranding from the colorwork is hidden inside the pocket created by double knitting. If you do not know how to double knit, there is a great class on Craftsy.com called "Adventures in Double Knitting with Alasdair Post-Quinn." You can learn all about the technique and how to knit both in the flat and in the round in this technique.

After watching me knit this piece up, my nine-year-old son requested I double knit him a bookmark with a cat motif, his favorite animal. I'm on it!

MATERIALS

Yarn: Knit Picks Gloss DK in Cranberry (MC) and Cream (CC) 70% Merino Wool, 30% Silk; 123 yards/50 g

Knitting needles: US size 6 (5 mm)

Notions

Tapestry needle

GAUGE

23 stitches over 4 inches

Gauge is important in this project. For more information on gauge, please refer to the section on gauge (page 8).

FINISHED MEASUREMENTS

6" x 2"

SKILLS NEEDED

You should be comfortable with double knitting.

TIPS

- In order to "seal up" the tube created by double knitting in the flat, you must twist the two yarns at the beginning of each row and perform a selvage stitch on the final pair at the end of each row.
- To perform the selvage stitch on the final pair, with yarn in back, slip the first stitch as if to purl. Move yarn to the front and slip the second stitch as if to purl through the back loop.
- For knitting abbreviations, see page 175.

INSTRUCTIONS

1. CO 33 pairs (not including the slipknot) with color MC as the front color and CC as the back color. Turn work.
2. Row 1: Following chart, (K1 MC wyib, P1 CC wyif) to second pair from the end (not including the slip knot). Work the selvage pair.
3. Row 2: Begin to work the chart. Remember to knit the first stitch in each pair with yarn in the back and the purl second stitch of each pair with yarn in front. Just follow the color indication on the chart. Note: Be very careful to follow the chart right to left for odd number rows and also right to left for even number rows.
4. Row 13: Bind off row. Bind off as you would normally except bind off in pairs. Knit the first pair as a unit. Knit the next pair. Slip the first pair from the right needle over the second pair on the right needle. One pair bound off. Continue until all stitches are bound off.
5. Weave ends into the inner pocket of the fabric.

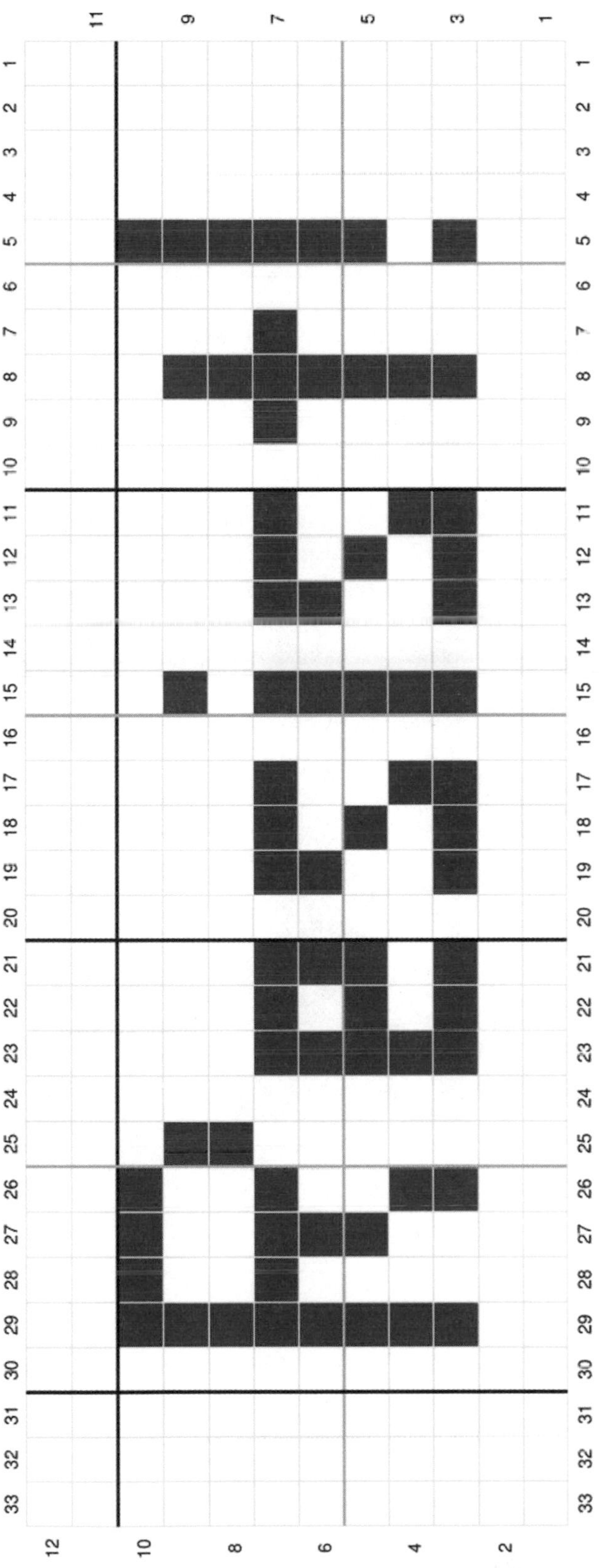

Girl Power Knitted Bath 'Mitt and Washcloth

By Heather Marano
Experience Level: Intermediate

Self-care is an important part of any movement. Sometimes we get so caught up in the work and so focused that we use all of our energy on the mission and have nothing left for ourselves. It's crucial to adopt self-care practices to help keep you grounded and energized.

Kathleen Ann Harper's book, The Well-Crafted Mom, *is a great read for helping you discover new ways to carve out time for yourself and create more happiness for your family.*

MATERIALS

Yarn: 1 ball each KnitPicks Dishie in Eggplant (MC) and Clarity (CC), 100% cotton; 190 yards/100 g worsted weight

½ yard of calico fabric of your choice

Knitting Needles: US size 8 (5 mm) double-pointed needles or two circular needles

Notions

Tapestry needle

Thread matching calico fabric

Straight pins

GAUGE

For both projects, 18 stitches and 26 rows = 4 inches

Gauge is important for this project. Please refer to the section on gauge and swatching (page 8).

FINISHED MEASUREMENTS

Bath Mitt: 8" x 6" (length x width)

Washcloths: 12" x 12"

TIPS

For knitting abbreviations, see page 175.

Bath Mitt

INSTRUCTIONS

1. With MC (eggplant), CO 40 stitches.

Ribbed Cuff

2. Place marker to indicate beginning of the round. Join in the round and begin to knit 1x1 (K1, P1) rib. Continue rib pattern until the piece measures 1½ inches from cast on edge. I worked my mitt using two circular needles, with 20 stitches on each needle. That made it easy to know where to place the increases and decreases. If you are working on DPNs, you will want to use stitch markers to keep track of the two halves of your mitt.

Body

3. Rounds 1: Knit with MC.
4. Round 2: K1, pm, K18, pm, K2, pm, K18, pm, K1. Join CC.

Increase Rounds

5. Round 3 and 4: With CC, K1, M1R, knit to marker, M1L, K1. 4 stitches increased, total of 44 stitches.
6. Round 5 and 6: With MC, K1, M1R, knit to marker, M1L, K1. 4 stitches increased, total of 48 stitches.
7. Repeat Rounds 3-5 two more times. 16 more stitches increased, total of 64 stitches.
8. Rounds 11 and 12: With CC, knit.
9. Rounds 13 and 14: With MC, knit.
10. Repeat rounds 11-14, continuing to alternate colors every two rounds until piece measures 6½ inches from cast on edge.

Decrease rounds

11. Next round: K1, ssk, knit to marker, K2tog, k2, ssk, knit to marker, K2tog, K1. 4 stitches decreased, total of 60 stitches.
12. Repeat round 11 with same color. 4 stitches decreased, total of 56 stitches.

13. Switch colors and repeat Rounds 11 and 12. 8 stitches decreased, total of 48 stitches.

14. Switch colors and repeat Rounds 11 and 12. 8 stitches decreased, total of 40 stitches.

15. Switch colors and repeat Rounds 11 and 12. 8 stitches decreased, total of 32 stitches.

16. Bind off. Weave in ends.

Washcloth

INSTRUCTIONS

1. Using the long tail cast on, CO 56 stitches.
2. Set up rows: knit 4 rows.
3. Row 1 (RS): Knit across row.
4. Row 2 (WS): K4, purl to last four stitches, K4.
5. Repeat rows 1 and 2 until piece measures 11½ inches from cast on edge.
6. Knit 3 rows.
7. Bind off final row (total of four knitted rows on this end).
8. Weave in ends.

Applique

1. Using the pattern, cut out your calico fabric.
2. Pin the applique to the washcloth using straight pins.
3. With coordinating thread, sew the applique to the washcloth. You may use a sewing machine or just topstitch it by hand. I did mine by hand, basting the stitches in first and then hand-stitching them nicely with just a running stitch.

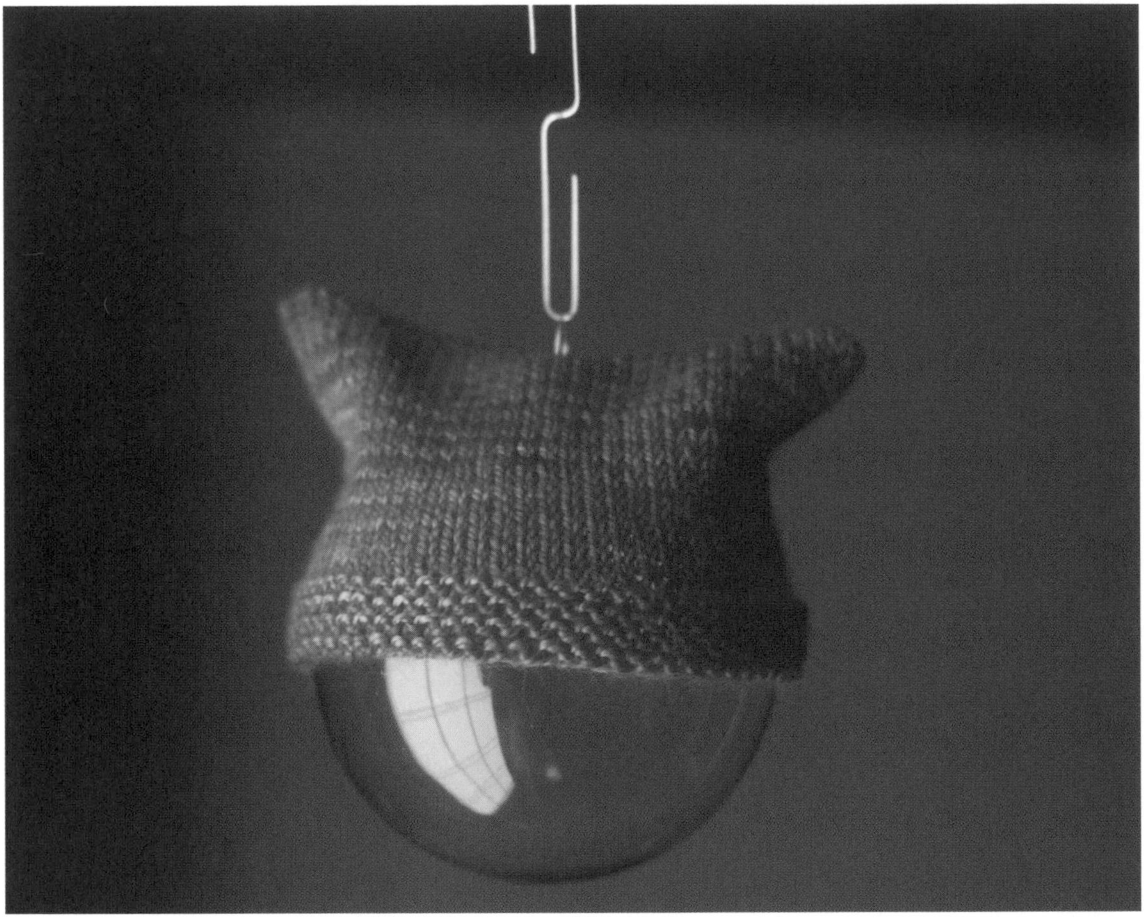

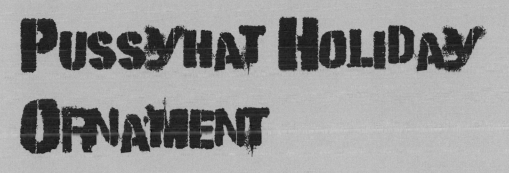

Pussyhat Holiday Ornament

by Lara Neel
Experience Level: Beginner

> Perhaps the very fact that Christmas has gone secular and commercial is directly related to the practical reality of its more recent implications. These might be the only real meaning Christmas has left. Children really are delighted by their gifts. Grown-ups really do enjoy watching their pleasure. The decorations really are pleasant to contemplate. The family feasts really are fun. The warmth of friends and relatives reaching out to one another really exists . . . Perhaps, after all, Christmas is not about gods or miraculous births or world-saving infants . . . Perhaps it is only about people.
>
> —Barbara G. Walker, *The Skeptical Feminist*

I'm not saying that you should read this quote to your deeply religious aunt over Christmas dinner, but I like Barbara Walker's take on the pleasure of Christmas and how it can extend to everyone, even if your relationship with religion is confusing, multi-faceted, or just plain complicated. I also think that this particular ornament doesn't have to be tied to Christmas. Use it anywhere (and anytime) you need a little dazzle! A person with a certain sense of humor might get a kick out of making these Pussyhat-themed holiday ornaments as gifts for "Don't You Know There's a War on Christmas" relatives.

The yarn for this project is a luxurious hand-dyed yarn by ModeKnit Yarn, which is the result of a lot of hard work and inspiring color choices by Annie Modesitt and Kathleen Pascuzzi. I can also highly recommend it for actual socks. Their bamboo and nylon content have kept the pair of socks I made from their yarn strong and beautiful through four Minnesota winters!

MATERIALS

Yarn: ModeKnit Yarns' ModeSock, 60% Super Wash Merino/30% Bamboo/10% Nylon; 382 yards/100 g per skein, in color A Study in Pink, 1 skein

Knitting needle: US size 3 (3.25 mm) double-pointed needles

Notions

3-inch-wide round glass ornament

Yarn needle

Stitch marker

GAUGE

27 stitches = 4 inches in stockinette stitch (see note on page 46 for tips on working a speed swatch)

FINISHED MEASUREMENTS

The Pussyhat is about 4.75" wide and 2.75" inches tall, when laid flat. It fits a glass ornament that is 3" wide.

TECHNIQUE

Three-Needle Bind Off
See page 47 for instructions.

TIPS

For knitting abbreviations, see page 175.

INSTRUCTIONS

1. Leaving a tail that is at least 6 inches long, CO 64 stitches.
2. Work 8 rows back and forth in garter stitch (knitting every stitch).
3. Being careful not to twist, join your knitting to work in the round. Place a marker for the beginning of the round.
4. Knit every stitch in each round until the pieces measures 2¾ inches high.
5. K16.
6. Turn your hat inside out.
7. Work a three-needle bind off.
8. Return to the long tail you left when you cast on and sew the small seam in the garter-stitch brim closed.
9. Weave in all ends and block gently, tugging on the ears so that they stand out well.
10. Pull the hat onto the glass ornament and gently guide the ornament's wire in between two stitches.

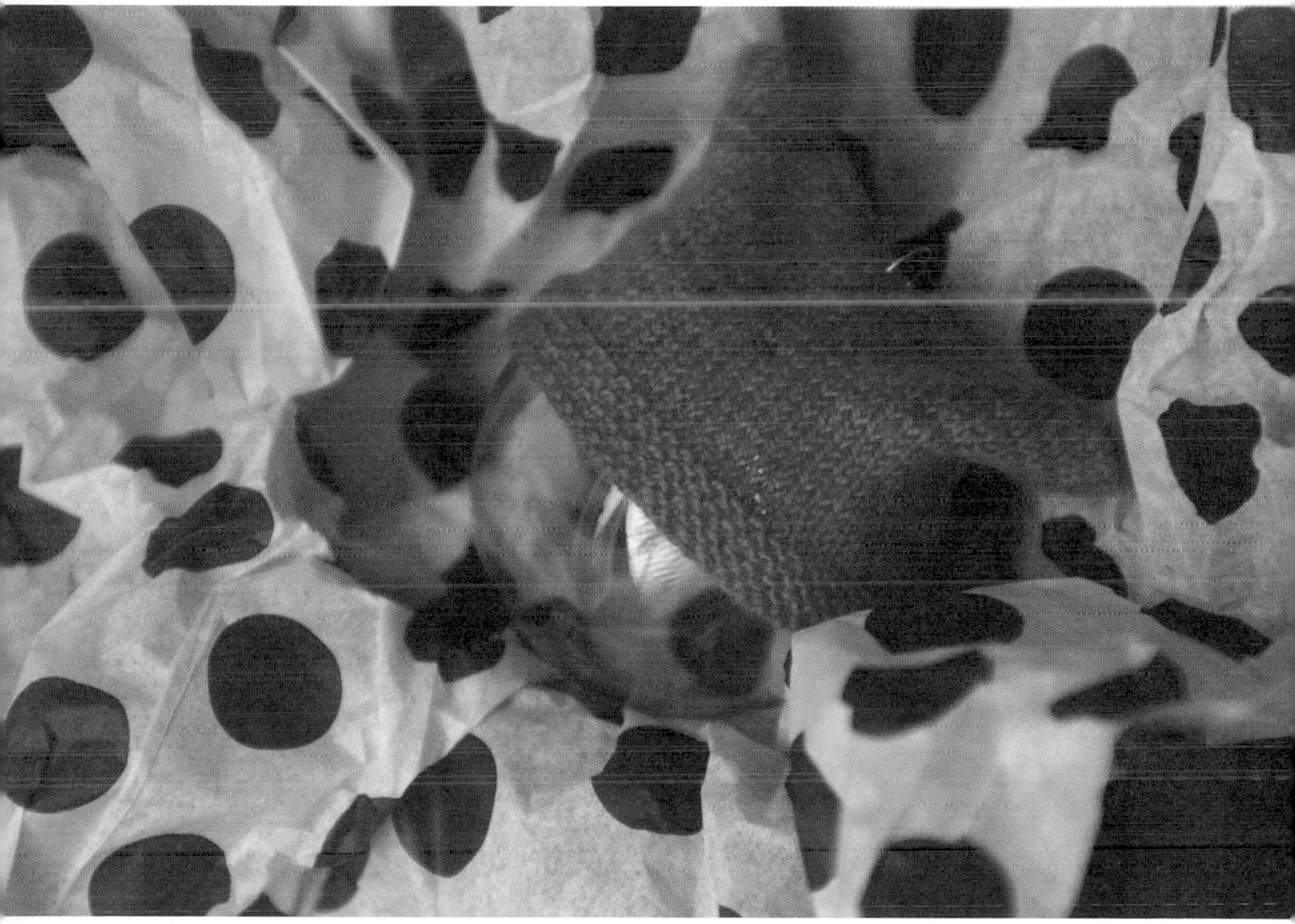

RESIST
PERSIST
RISE
STRENGTH

RESIST FELTED RUG

by Heidi Harris of West County Fiber Arts

Experience Level: Beginner

My path of joining the Resistance started when Hillary Clinton was unfairly portrayed as not the most educated or qualified candidate for President. My rage needed to be heard, so I protested the Electoral College vote at my state capitol and proudly wore my Pussyhat. My hat was made with a group of like women at our local yarn store, Cast Away. Nothing gave me more strength than to be an example for my two daughters. I want to be on the right side of history voicing my opinion. This movement is against hate and ignorance and the absolute conviction of caring for every one of my neighbors as human beings. As a people, we must look after our elders and children—be the voice of those that are too weak or strong to have one. We share this planet with all life because we know better—and we should do better.

There are three parts to making this rug. The first is to make a base/the actual shape of the rug. I use a wine barrel metal ring as the mold. I put all the wool in the mold and wet felt first. After the base is felted, I then needle felt the message on top of the base and wet felt one more time so the needle felting message becomes part of the rug.

By using natural or colored roving you may add color and texture to create a rug that will be the center of attention in any room. For this project, you will use about 1 pound of wool and learn the techniques to create this very strong, warm, nonwoven cloth that is created by matting, condensing, and pressing the fibers. It is labor-intensive, but you will love the result.

FINISHED MEASUREMENTS

26" in diameter

MATERIALS

16 oz merino wool top or wool roving for the main color

2 pieces of bubble wrap roughly the same size as the rug you'll be making

1 tutu net or mesh fabric such as tulle, roughly the same size as the rug

Bamboo mat or something you can roll around your piece to agitate the fibers

Clean, plastic 1 quart milk container with holes punched in the lid

Bar of soap and liquid soap

Vinegar

Metal ring, such as one from a wine barrel. If no metal rings are available, you can approximate the size of the circle you want as you lay down your first layer of wool. It will be more challenging to shape the sides without a ring but it can be done.

INSTRUCTIONS

Preparation

1. First, prepare the surface you will be working on. If you are a visual person, "Wet felting 4- laying out the wool" by Teri Pike[2] is a great YouTube video on preparing the surface and layout of your wool.

2 Pike, Teri, "Wet felting 4- laying out the wool," YouTube.com. https://www.youtube.com/watch?v=3nFY4AACYs0

2. Lay down the bubble wrap with the bubbles facing up. The surface of the bubble wrap needs to be a bit larger than the piece you are felting. If you need to, tape two pieces of bubble wrap together using duct tape on the smooth side. Remember your project is going to shrink to about two-thirds the size of your initial layout of wool. Measure the size you want, and mark those dimensions with tape on the bubble wrap.

Drafting/Laying Out the Wool

3. Take your round metal ring and place it on the middle of the bubble wrap.

4. Start drafting your wool; gently pull off palm sized tufts of wool. Take your roving and start laying it down inside the ring in one direction, overlaying each tuft in the same direction till you get one layer. You want to create the first layer in the size of your finished piece. Remember: many thin layers of wool are much better than only a few thick layers.

5. Create a second layer on top, placing the wool in the opposite direction. Do a third layer going in the original direction, and then a fourth layer in the opposite direction, so you have four layers of wool. Laying the wool out in opposite directions will allow the wool layers to attach together more easily. Press down on your

project to see if you feel any thin spots and correct those by adding more tufts to those areas.

6. Now it's time to decide how you want your piece to look by adding different colors of roving or adding embellishments. If you want to add needle felted words or sayings, you must felt the base first.

Wet Felting

In this process, you are facilitating the binding and cohesion of the separate fibers into one solid fabric by doing three things: *opening up the fibers* so they bind together using heat, *removing air* by adding water so the fibers settle in and mingle together to help the binding process, and *massaging the fibers* using soap so that they slide and connect to one another and smooth into a consistent thickness.

7. Keeping your design in place, carefully place a mesh screen over the top of your project.

8. Pour warm water into your quart plastic jar and pour the water onto the wool in a circular motion until all areas are completely soaked with water. There should not be any puddles of water. Gently press your flat hands down on the wool to take out the air. Run your flat palms over the surface, smoothing out any wrinkles by pressing gently into the wool, encouraging the fibers to bind. Continue to press your hands on the screen, then add a little soap to your hands and start working in a small circular motion for a short time. Slowly remove the screen.

9. There may be wool that has worked through the screen—gently pull up the screen to detach them. Occasionally lift your screen and move it so the wool doesn't bind to the screen.

10. Gently rub in any bumps or wrinkles. Continue to do this step until you feel the wool is integrated and thickening in all areas, massaging it so that the fibers are settling in and binding with one another, but not so hard that you are pushing the fibers around and disrupting your design. If you still feel any areas that don't seem flat and compact, there's more work to do.

11. You'll know you've finished this process of felting when you can push gently on the fiber and it does not give or move under your fingers. You can also check the underside to see that the wool fibers have woven through and are slightly visible on the other side. At this point it has become a cohesive fabric. The final test is to pinch the surface of the wool with your fingers and lift up. If individual fibers come up, then it's not ready. If they are all bound together and your pinch pulls up the whole piece as one, it's complete and ready for fulling.

Fulling

In this process, you are tightening the bonds created in the felting process and strengthening the fabric by shrinking it, further removing the space between the fibers. In fulling, agitate the felted material using either bamboo mats, or something that has resistance. You will use pressure, gravity, and force.

12. Place a bamboo mat onto a flat surface and place your piece on top. Arrange it so that the bamboo mat is parallel with the edge of your work surface. If you do not have a bamboo mat, you can use a thin PVC pipe and roll your piece up around it in bubble wrap. You may also use a pool noodle cut to size for your project. Keep in mind the pool noodle is not as firm and might take more passes to complete the process.

13. Begin rolling up the mat and your felt together into a tight roll and, with your palms, add pressure and roll it back and forth, as if you were rolling out dough with a rolling pin, rolling it from your palms to your elbows. Do this rolling motion 30 times.

14. Unroll the mat and turn your fabric 90 degrees on the mat. Roll it back up and repeat the rolling process another 30 times.

15. Continue rotating and rolling until it is clear that the felt is bound tightly together and strong, at least two more times per side. You will be able to see that this process is shrinking and strengthening the fabric.

16. Remove your piece from the bamboo mat. Compact the piece into a ball in your hands and throw it down onto your work surface. This is called striking and it feels really good to throw your piece down and slam it against the table for several minutes. This locks the fibers and makes it solid. Pick it up and repeat, for 5 minutes.

Rinsing and Drying

17. In a bucket, add ¼ cup vinegar per 1 gallon of room temperature water, and place your piece in the bucket. Rinse until the water running through is no longer soapy.

18. Place over a drying rack or hang up to dry.

Adding Felt Words

19. Take a felting needle and a piece of foam and start to write your message of *RESIST* on the front. After you have finished your message, you can put roving or color on your piece.

Repeat the Process

20. Finally, repeat the Wet Felting Process to the Rinsing and Drying Process to fully adhere your message to the rug.

Resistance Ornaments

By Donna Druchunas

Skill Level: Intermediate

Sometimes, many small statements make as much impact as one big statement. These ornaments are quick projects that can be made in an evening. Print out signs with your favorite sayings about migrant justice, climate change, or other social justice issues, and hang one up on each public bulletin board where you live. Even if you can't make it to a big march, or knit a hundred Pussyhats, this is one small way to help love trump hate in your own town.

MATERIALS

Yarn: Red Heart Supersaver, 100% acrylic; 364 yards/333 m per 200 g skein

Each ornament uses about 10 yards (9 m) of 2 colors (MC and CC)

Additional yard of black for duplicate stitch on the butterfly ornament

Knitting needles: US size 8 (5 mm) circular needles 16 inches (40 cm) long and DPNs *or* 1 long circular needle *or* 2 short circular needles for working in the round

Notions

Tapestry needle

Fiberfill or extra yarn for stuffing

GAUGE

20 stitches and 28 rounds = 4 inches in stockinette stitch

Exact gauge is not critical for this project, but be sure your stitches are tight enough that the stuffing does not show through or pop out. Please refer to page 8 for more information on gauge and swatching.

FINISHED MEASUREMENTS

Approximately 5.5" tall

TECHNIQUES

I-cord

You will need two double-pointed needles of the same size you used for the project.

1. On the first needle, CO the specified number of stitches from the pattern. For this pattern, that is 3 stitches. *Do not turn the work.*
2. Slide the stitches to the other end of the needle.
3. Now the right side is facing you. Bring the working yarn behind and knit into those stitches. *Do not turn the work.*
4. Slide the stitches to the other end of the needle and knit again.
5. Continue in this fashion, never turning the work but sliding the stitches to the other end of the needle each time.
6. When you've knitted the desired or specified length of I-cord, bind off as usual.

Duplicate Stitch

This technique allows you to add different colors onto your already knitted piece. It is a great technique to have if you want to correct an error in a stranded colorwork piece!

You will need the yarn you are stitching with and a tapestry needle.

1. Thread your tapestry needle with the yarn you'll be stitching with.
2. From the back, insert the needle into bottom of the "v" of the stitch you are covering. Pull the yarn through.
3. Follow the line of the stitch and put the needle back through the top of the stitch. (The row above which you are adding your duplicate stitch.)
4. Take the needle under both legs (the full stitch) in this row.
5. Insert the needle back in where you came out originally.
6. Insert the needle under both legs (the full stitch) of the row *below* the stitch you are duplicating. The needle is now in front. This completes the duplication of one stitch.
7. Repeat steps 2–6 for all stitches that need duplicate stitch.

TIPS

For knitting abbreviations, see page 175.

INSTRUCTIONS

1. With MC, CO 4 stitches. Join to work in the round, being careful not to twist.
2. Knit all rounds, following chart. Tie knots in the yarn, leaving a 4-inch (10cm) tail when attaching a new color. There is no need to weave in ends on this project.
3. After round 27, steam block the ornament, allow to dry, then stuff.
4. When chart is complete, 4 stitches remain. Put all stitches on 1 DPN or short circular needle.
5. Next row: K1, K2tog, K1; 3 stitches remain.

Finishing

1. Work 3-stitch I-cord for 2 inches. Bind off. Sew the end of the I-cord to base of cord to form a loop.
2. For butterfly, work black in duplicate stitch.
3. Bury ends inside ornament.

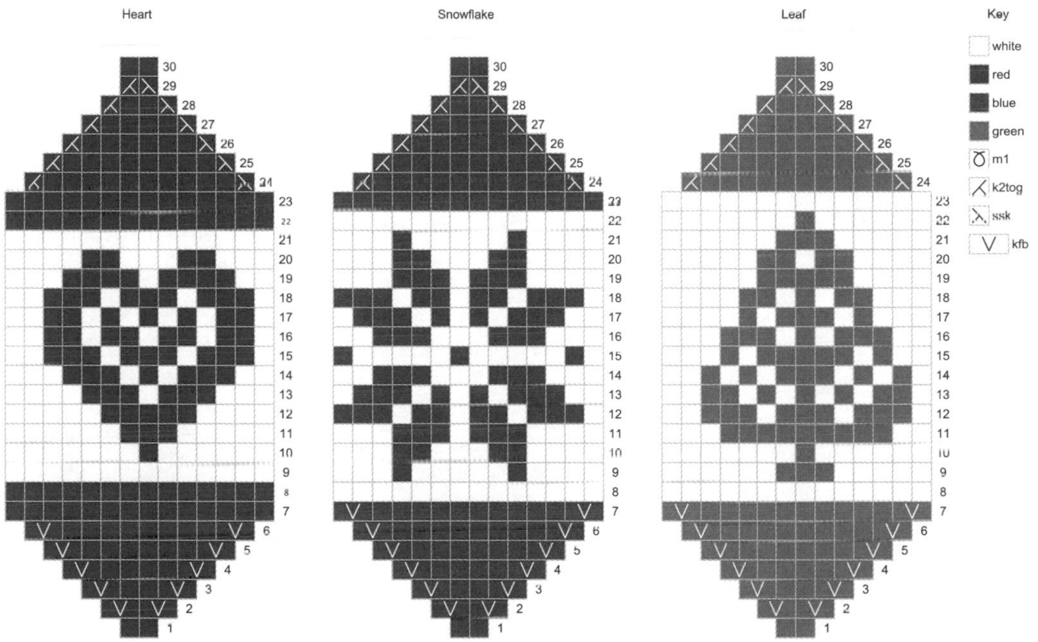

The political core of any movement for freedom in the society has to have the political imperative to protect free speech.

—bell hooks

Around Town

HeForShe Coffee Cup Cozy

by Heather Marano

Experience Level: Intermediate

The inspiration for this design is the United Nations Women's Organization, which stands and fights for gender equality around the world. This is their logo and a great way to show you are HeForShe. Learn more about what HeForShe is doing worldwide and how you can help at www.heforshe.org. You can get creative with this pattern by adapting it to fit any logo you like.

MATERIALS

Yarn: Knit Picks Gloss DK, 70% Merino/30% Silk, in Cream (MC), Cranberry (CC1), and Navy (CC2); 123 yards/50 g each ball

Knitting needles: US size 6 (4 mm) straight needles

Notions

Tapestry needle

7 bobbins

GAUGE

24 stitches and 32 rows over 4 inches. 6 stitches = 1 inch.

SKILLS NEEDED

Knit, purl, intarsia, mattress stitch

TECHNIQUES

Intarsia

This cozy uses intarsia for the red-and-navy design. Using stranded colorwork would create very long floats across the back. Intarsia eliminates those floats, creating a nicer fabric with less puckering. The red and navy colors will be on bobbins and as you follow the chart, you simply knit from the color identified on the chart. The yarn is not carried behind the work but simply left hanging at the end of each color segment. Be sure to twist your two yarns together before each color change. Otherwise you will end up with your intarsia design only attached at the top and the bottom but floating free on the sides.

Mattress Stitch

First, line up the two ends to face each other. Try to get all the stitches on the sides to line up with each other. You will be creating the seam with these.

1. Thread a tapestry needle with the tail of your yarn from the cast on edge.
2. Insert the needle from front to back between the first and second stitches on the opposite side (from the one with the tail) and pull the yarn through.
3. Return to the other side (the side with the tail) and insert the needle from front to back where the yarn previously came out of the piece. Slip the needle upward under the next horizontal bar and bring the needle through to the front.
4. Move to the other side and repeat the process, going from front to back where you came out the last time, and coming under one bar and up to the front again.
5. Repeat until seam is complete and then weave in the remains of the tail.

TIPS

For knitting abbreviations, see page 175.

INSTRUCTIONS

1. Begin by winding two bobbins each with red, three bobbins with white, and two bobbins each with dark navy.
2. With MC, CO 46 stitches. Work 5 rows of knit 1x1 (K1, P1) rib.
3. (RS) Knit 1 row.
4. (WS) Purl 1 row.
5. (RS) Knit 1 row.
6. (WS) Purl 1 row.
7. Work rows 1 through 15 of chart.
8. (WS) Row 16 Knit.
9. (RS) Row 17 Purl.
10. (WS) Row 18 Knit.
11. (RS) Row 19 Purl.
12. Work 5 rows of knit 1x1 (K1, P1) rib.
13. Bind off in ribbing pattern.

Finishing

14. Weave in all ends then block. Soak in water and spread flat to dry. Using mattress stitch, sew up the two sides.

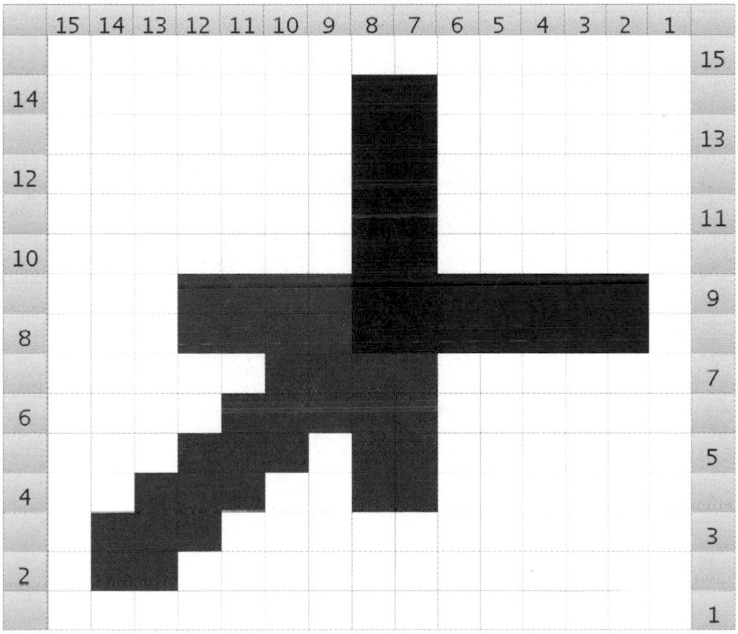

RESISTANCE COWL

by Heather Marano
Experience Level: Intermediate

Resistance isn't just about marching in protests, it's also about going against the rules, going against the dogma. One of the primary rules about knitting in the round is to be extra certain when joining the first row that your stitches are not twisted. Twisted stitches lead to a faux Moebius band which, if you are making a hat, will make you very sad. True Moebius knitting is way more involved in terms of the cast on and how the piece is knit. This faux version is easy, and produces a fun result. Whip it up in a self-striping or multiyarn for an effortless statement piece. This one is so easy to work it's great to do while watching TV or listening to an audiobook (my favorite way to knit!).

Just for extra fun, this pattern of knit and purl rows is based on the Fibonacci sequence. This sequence of numbers begins: 0, 1, 1, 2, 3, 5, 8, 13, 21, 34 . . . . The next number in the sequence is found by adding the two numbers before it. This is a fun sequence to use for two-color pattern work as well.

MATERIALS

Yarn: Lorna's Laces Shepherd Worsted 100% Superwash Merino Wool, 3 skeins in color Wild Turkey; 225 yards/4 oz per skein

Knitting needles: US size 6 (4 mm) 24-inch-long circular needles

Notions

Tapestry needle

Stitch marker

GAUGE

20 stitches = 4 inches blocked; however, gauge is not necessary for this project

SKILLS NEEDED

Cast on, knit, purl, and knit and purl in the round

TECHNIQUE

Faux Moebius

After casting on the required number of stitches, line up both needles and prepare to join in the round. Make a twist of 180 degrees on the stitches on *one* of the needles. Then knit the setup round. There should now be a single twist in the piece which will look like a Moebius when the project is complete.

TIPS

For knitting abbreviations, see page 175.

INSTRUCTIONS

1. CO 170 stitches.
2. Following the Faux Moebius technique, introduce the single twist and then join in the round and knit the set-up round. Place a stitch marker at the beginning of the round.
3. Row 1: Knit all stitches.
4. Row 2: Purl all stitches.
5. Rows 3–4: Knit all stitches.
6. Rows 5–7: Purl all stitches.
7. Rows 8–12: Knit all stitches.
8. Rows 13–20: Purl all stitches.
9. Rows 21–33: Knit all stitches.
10. Rows 34–54: Purl all stitches.
11. Rows 55–88: Knit all stitches.

Finishing

12. Bind off all stitches. Weave in ends. Block.

PARK

Pussyhat Bombs

by Lara Neel

Experience Level: Beginner

> The kind of activity that is built into the traditional female role is different in quality from masculine activity. Masculine activity (repairing a window, building a house) tends to be sporadic, concrete, and to have a finished product. Feminine activity (comforting a crying child, preparing a meal, washing laundry) tends to be repetitive, less tangible, and to have no final durable product. Here again our sense of inferiority came into place. We had come to think of our activity as doing nothing—although it was essential for maintaining life—and of male activity as superior...as women we have been taught to want to fail, or if not to fail, to walk a fine line between success and failure. We were never encouraged to use our full strength . . .
>
> —*Our Bodies, Ourselves* by The Boston Women's Health Collective, Inc. (1976 edition)

I would argue that crafting allows people of all genders to inhabit a space in between masculine and feminine work. It can be soothingly repetitive and, usually, creates a physical finished product. It is true that knitting, sewing, crochet, and other types of soft crafts have recently been coded as "women's work," but they don't have to be. Knitting, for example, only became part of a housewife's duties when it was no longer a guild-guarded form of waged work. Perhaps perversely, I feel closest to the ambiguously-gendered nature of crafting when I think about using crafts to transform a public space.

I'm not advocating actually bombing anything, but you might enjoy reading Complete Hothead Paisan: Homicidal Lesbian Terrorist *by Diane DiMassa as you contemplate turning sewing scraps into little Pussyhats to leave behind in your wake.*

MATERIALS

Scraps of pink fleece

Notions

Matching all-purpose thread

Basic sewing kit

Walking foot

FINISHED MEASUREMENTS

These will vary, depending on the size of your scraps.

INSTRUCTIONS

1. Trim away any flaws in scraps and make sure the corners are square.
2. If a piece is wide, but not tall, measure its length. Take the length, divide it by 2, and add 1 inch. This is the width you should use. You may be able to cut more than one. If a piece is tall, but not terribly wide, measure its width. Take the width, subtract 1 inch, and multiply the result by 2. This is the length you should use. You may be able to cut more than one.
3. Fold each piece, right sides together, so that the two short sides meet.
4. Stitch up the sides with a ½-inch seam allowance.
5. Turn up the hem. Press down the center of the hat until it is a shape you like.

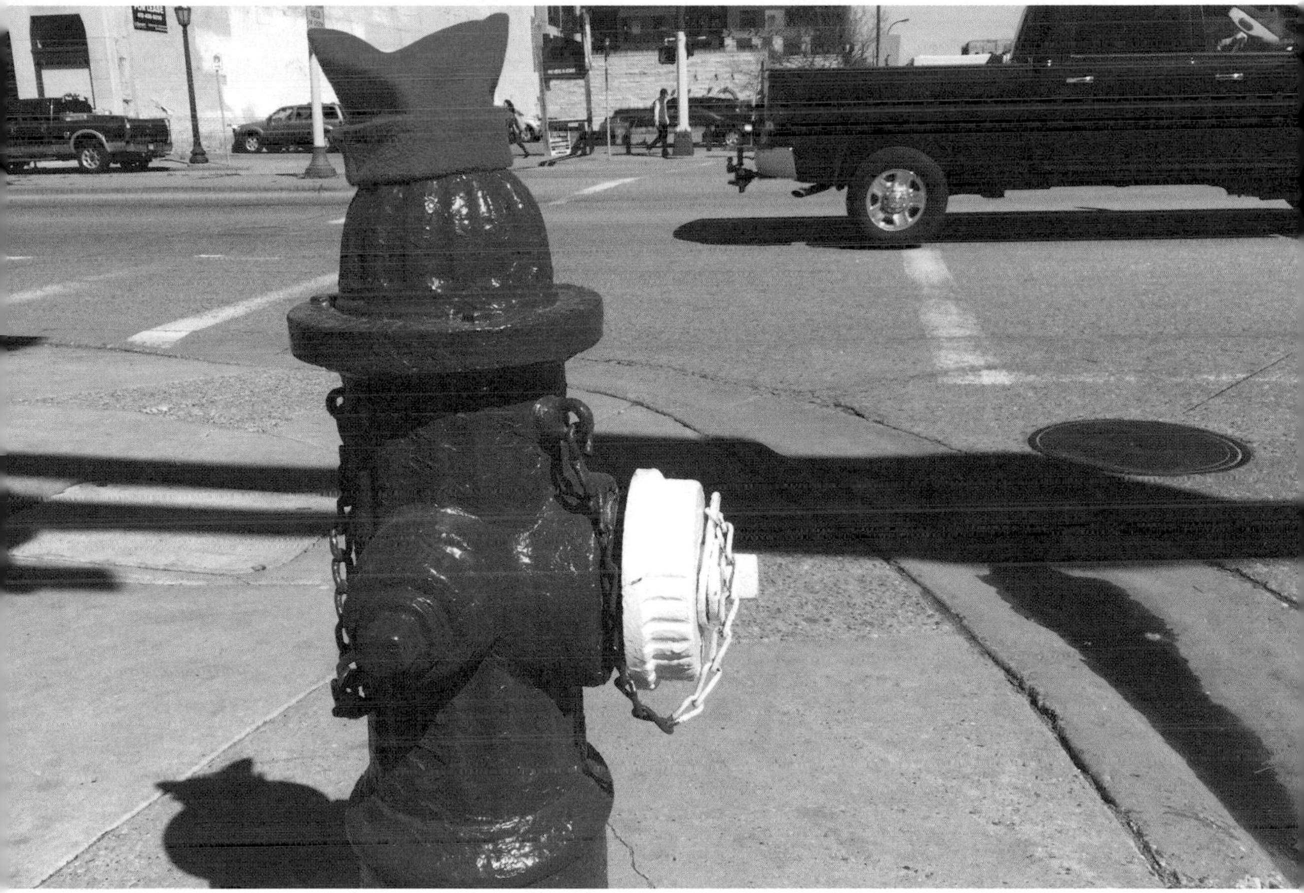

Jabot-Inspired Scarf

by Lara Neel
Experience Level: Beginner

Before Ruth Bader Ginsburg became "The Notorious RBG," I doubt that many people outside of the legal profession had heard of a jabot. Now, there are entire online photo galleries of Ginsburg's extensive collection. She uses her jabots to make visual statements. There's one just for when she dissents and another for when she reads the majority opinion. I like to think she would enjoy it if you wore this scarf when channeling her fierce, smart ability to take on the world.

MATERIALS

½ yard of white shirting fabric

3½ yards of white lace (see Tips)

Notions

Matching all-purpose thread

Pins

Applique scissors

Tear-away stabilizer (optional, see Tips)

FINISHED MEASUREMENTS

About 16" wide and as long as your fabric is wide.

TIPS

- Make sure the lace you choose does not stretch. It can be any style, but it should be at least 1 inch wide.
- Keep your hands clean. White fabric stains easily! I like to wash my hands before I start sewing and any time I open the bobbin case.
- Applique scissors will make trimming easier.
- Not every machine can handle stitching over lace, especially when the supporting fabric is loosely woven. If your machine doesn't feed smoothly, cut stabilizer into 1-inch strips and place them between your project and the feed dogs.

CUTTING INSTRUCTIONS

If the selvedge of your shirting piece lies flat, leave the selvedge in place. Otherwise, trim it off and hem it as for the ends of the lace.

Square off the cut ends of your shirting piece.

Lace will be cut to measure during construction.

INSTRUCTIONS

1. If needed, hem the short edges of the shirting fabric by turning them to the wrong side ¼ inch, then turning them under again. Stitch in place. If you chose not to trim away your selvedge, skip this step.
2. Cut 2 pieces of lace, each as long as your fabric is wide, plus 1 inch.
3. Turn the cut end of your lace under ¼ inch, then under again. Stitch in place. Repeat on all cut edges of lace.
4. Place your lace right-side up, aligning the edge of the lace with the raw edge of the wrong side of the fabric. Allow any scallops in the lace to hang off the edge of the fabric. Pin in position.

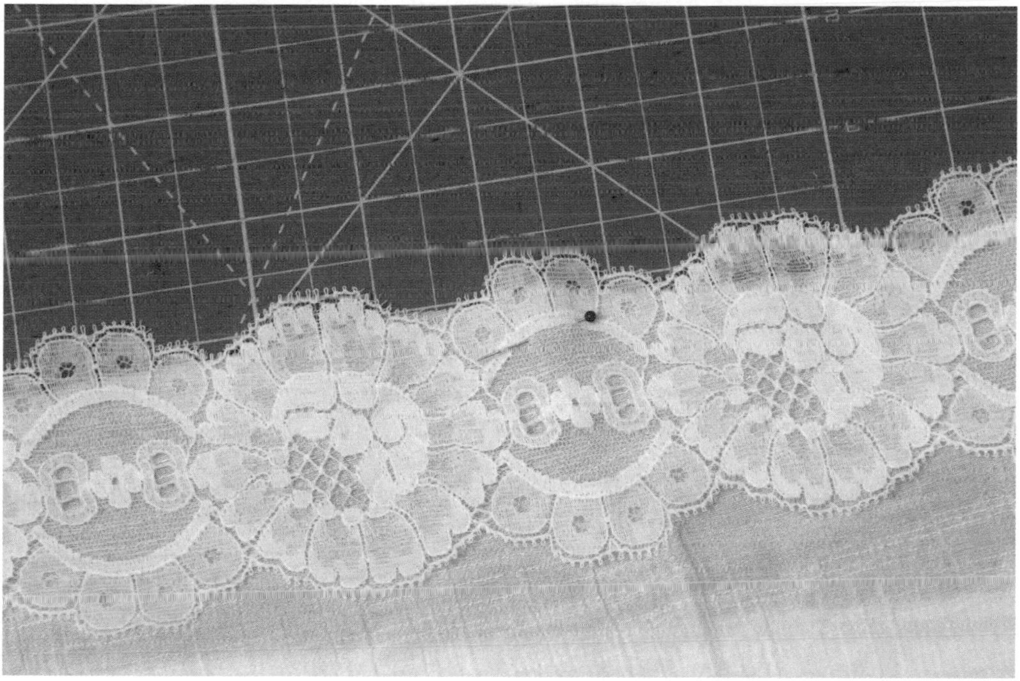

5. Stitch, with the lace on top, about ½ inch from the fabric's edge. Keep your eye on the position of the needle relative to the lace and keep it as even as possible.
6. Trim away all but ¼ inch of the fabric's seam allowance, taking care not to cut the lace.
7. Turn the lace to the right side, enclosing the fabric's raw edge. Topstitch the lace in position, ⅜ inch from the folded edge of the fabric.
8. Repeat steps 2–7 for the other side of the scarf.

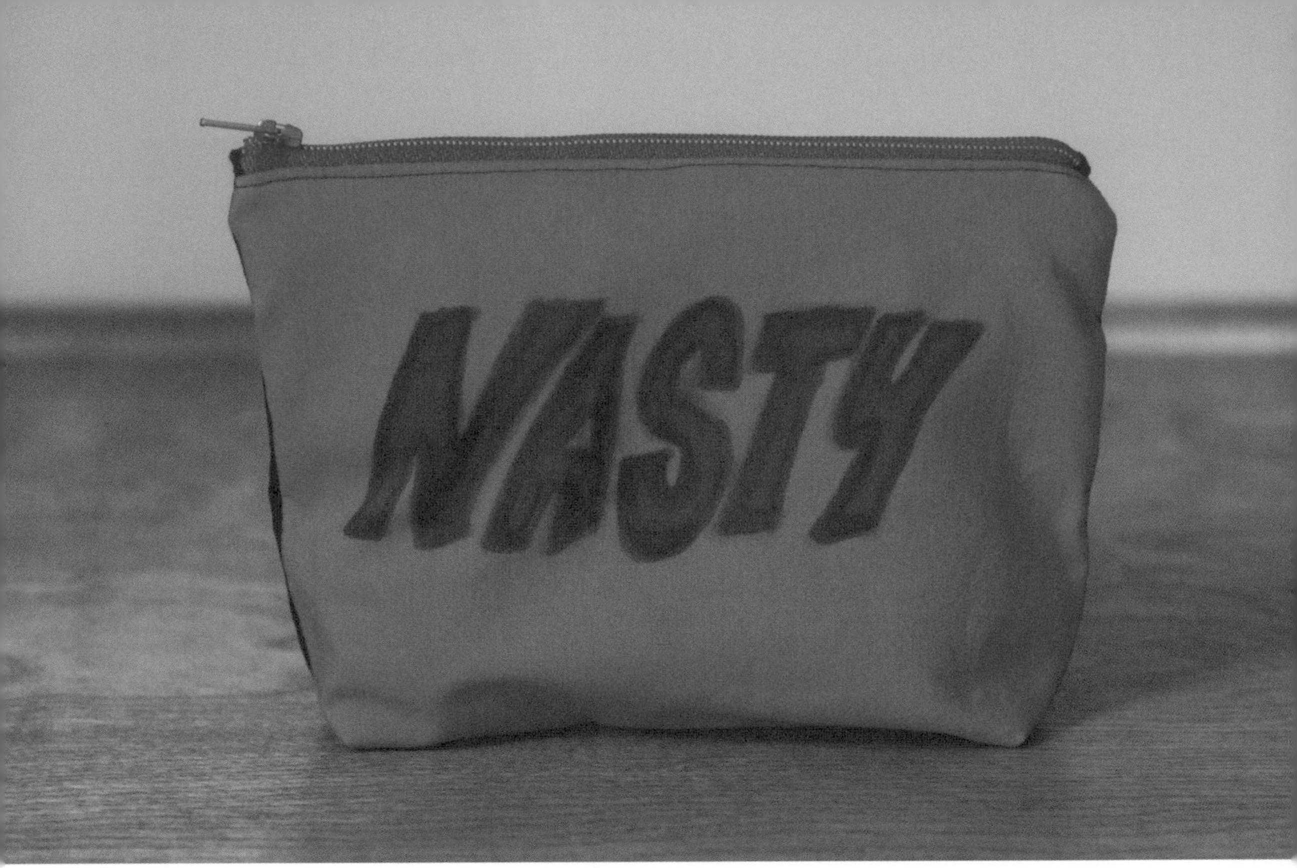
NASTY

Call Congress
202-224-3121

Nasty Nag Pouch

by Lara Neel

Experience Level: Beginner

We all need a little push now and again. This pouch includes a window where you can place a note to yourself. The note could be a to-do list, an affirmation, or anything else you think you will need that day. I made it a little stiff, so that it can stand up on its own, as a reminder. You could put your phone in it, but there's also room for all of the little things you might need throughout the day. Or, just fill it with a ton of little notes and rotate them!

My friend Cindy Laun hand-lettered "Nasty" for this project. As someone who has terrible handwriting, I'm very, very grateful to her.

MATERIALS

¼ yard or a fat quarter of black cotton fabric (see Tips)

¼ yard or a fat quarter of pink cotton fabric

¼ yard or a fat quarter of lining fabric (see Tips)

¼ yard of Pellon® SF101 Shape-Flex fusible interfacing

Scrap of pink felt

Scrap of vinyl

Notions

Basic sewing kit

7-inch-long zipper

Matching all-purpose thread

Iron-on transfer pen

Tracing paper

Permanent fabric marker

Zipper foot

Walking foot

Standard foot

Rotary cutter

Self-healing mat

Chalk marker

Straight pins

Jeans or leather needle

Standard sewing machine needle

Washaway Wonder Tape (optional)

Patternmaking supplies or photocopier

FINISHED MEASUREMENTS

7.5" x 5" (width x height)

TIPS

- I like quilting cotton for this project. If you want to use a heavier cotton fabric, like duck or canvas, you might not need to use interfacing.
- I used an old bed sheet for the lining fabric.
- Use any color you like for this project, but I do have a word of warning. I made a bag with white zipper end covers and I thought they looked fantastic for about three weeks. Now, I still like the bag, but the zipper ends look a little grubby. So, unless you wash your hands every 5 minutes, you might want to steer clear of light-colored fabric for that part of your bag.

CUTTING INSTRUCTIONS

Pieces without patterns:

Main pieces: 8.5" x 6.5"
Interfacing pieces: 8" x 6"
Zipper end cover: 5.5" x 2.5"

Cut one main piece in black fabric.

Cut one main piece in pink fabric.

Cut two main pieces in lining fabric.

Cut two interfacing pieces

Cut one zipper end cover piece.

Cut a window in felt using the pattern piece (page 151), then cut out the center of the window.

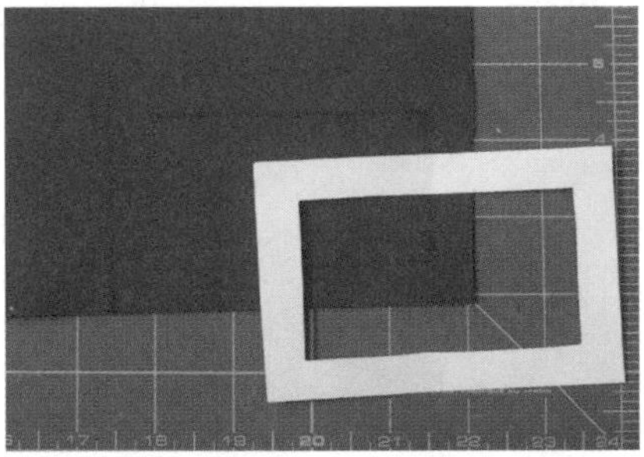

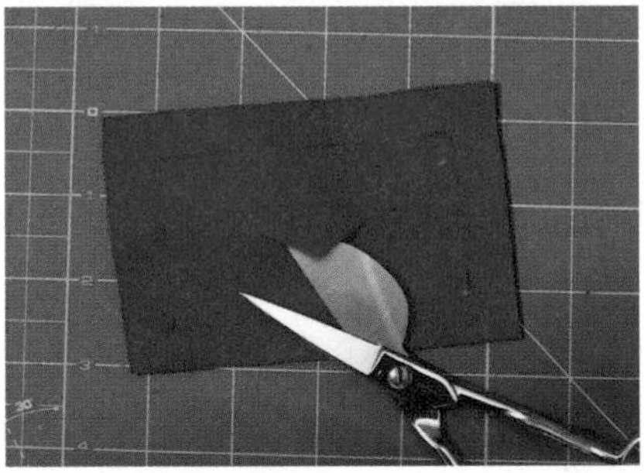

Cut a piece of heavy vinyl that is the same size as the window (you can use shears for this, but it's easier with a rotary cutter and mat).

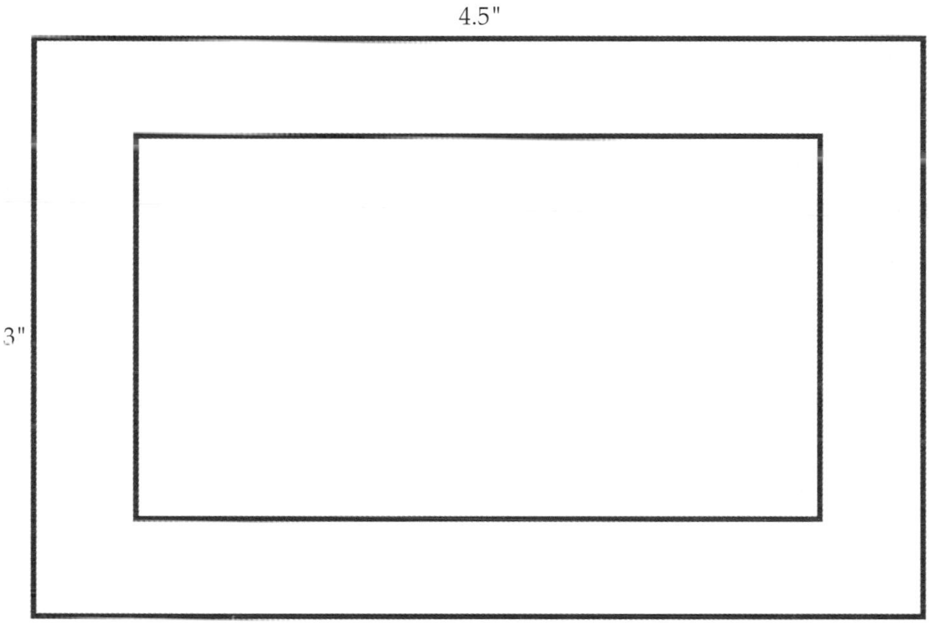

Pg 151: Window, with 0.5" border

YES NO
NASTY
YES NO
NASTY

YES NO
NASTY
YES no
nasty

INSTRUCTIONS

1. Use the iron-on transfer pen to trace the "Nasty" template (pages 152–153) onto tracing paper. Make sure you're tracing the version that is mirror-imaged to the final product you want (it appears to look backwards). We've included both versions here, as well as the other words "Yes" and "No" in case you decide to use the original image for another project.

2. Following the instructions that came with your pen, transfer the lettering onto the pink side of your bag.

3. Outline the transfer using a permanent fabric marker. Fill the letters in, too, if you like.

4. Following the instructions that came with your interfacing, fuse it to the back of your main bag pieces.

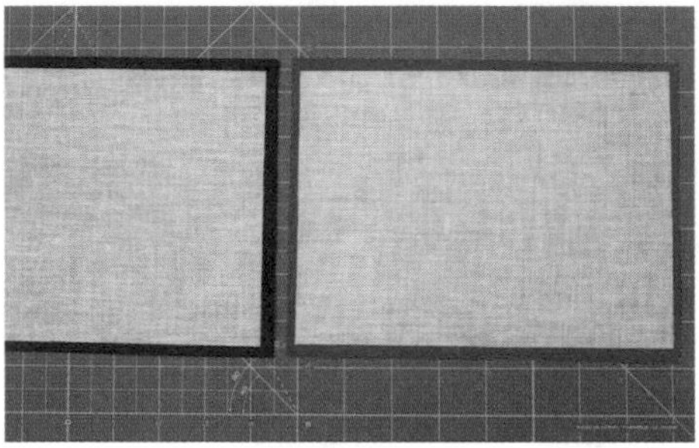

5. Using your walking foot and a jeans or leather needle, stitch the felt window to the piece of vinyl, working as close to the inside edge of the window as possible.

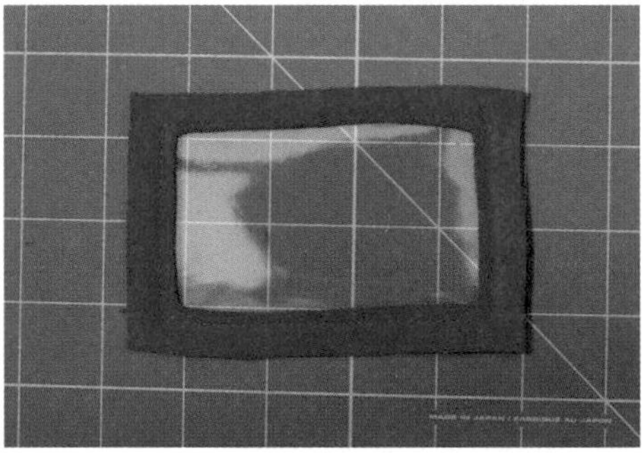

6. Stitch again, close to the top edge of the window.

7. Stitching may have pushed your window slightly out of shape. If any vinyl is sticking out from underneath the window, trim it away.

8. Position your window about ½ inch higher than the center of your main black piece. Working as close to the outside edge of the window as possible, attach the window to the piece by stitching down one side, across the bottom, then up the other side. If you have trouble keeping the window in place, use Washaway Wonder Tape to secure it before you stitch.

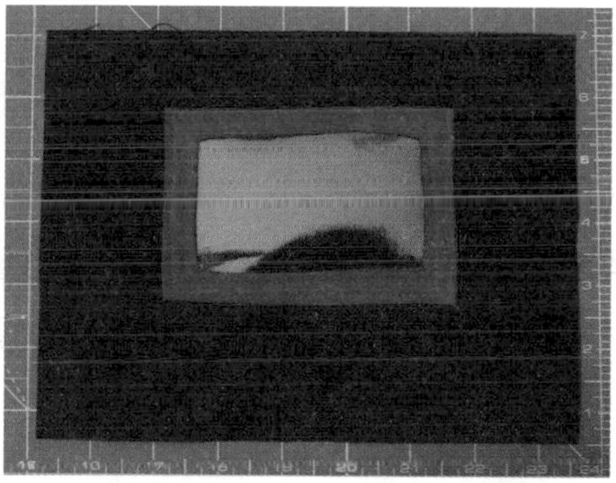

9. Fold the zipper end piece in half, lengthwise, and press it. Cut it in half.

10. Using your zipper foot, attach a zipper end piece to each end of your zipper, stitching as close to the ends of the zipper as possible.

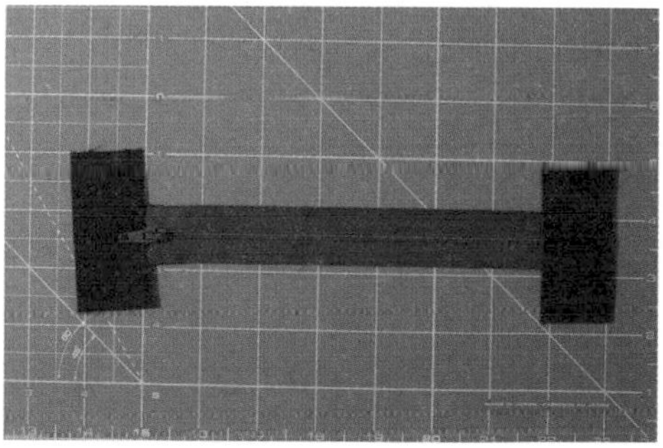

11. Place a lining piece right-side up, your zipper right-side up, and a main piece wrong-side up. Align the raw edges, allowing the zipper end pieces to stick out. Stitch close to the zipper teeth.

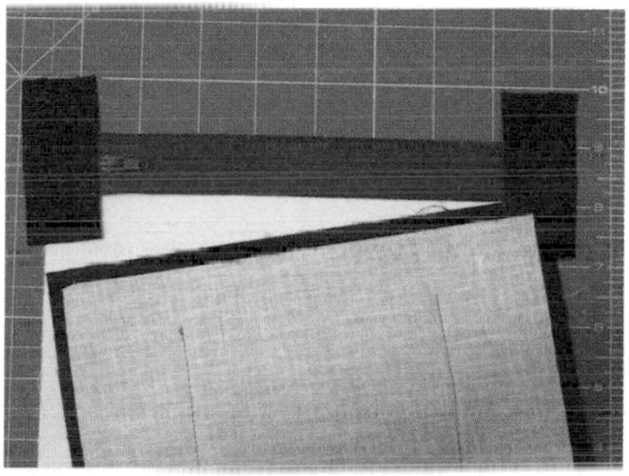

12. Press the lining and main pieces, wrong sides together, away from the zipper. Be careful not to touch the zipper teeth or the vinyl window with the iron.

13. Place the other lining piece right-side up, your zipper right-side up, and the other main piece wrong-side up. Align the raw edges, allowing the zipper end pieces to stick out. Stitch close to the zipper teeth.

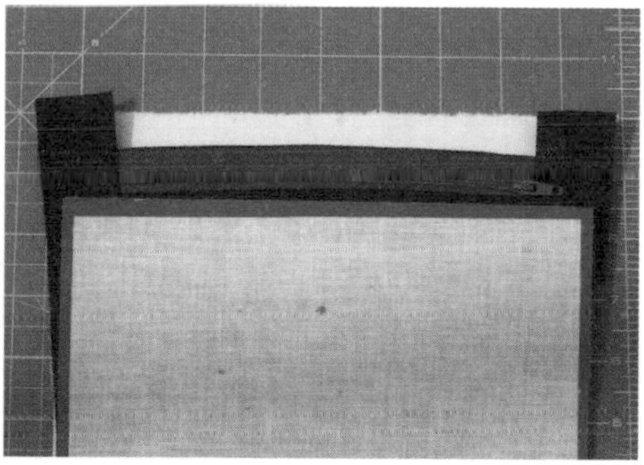

14. Press the lining and main pieces, wrong sides together, away from the zipper. Be careful not to touch the zipper teeth or the vinyl window with the iron.

15. Topstitch through all layers on each side, close to the zipper.

16. Unzip the zipper. Fold the work so that the lining pieces have their right sides together and the main pieces have their right sides together.

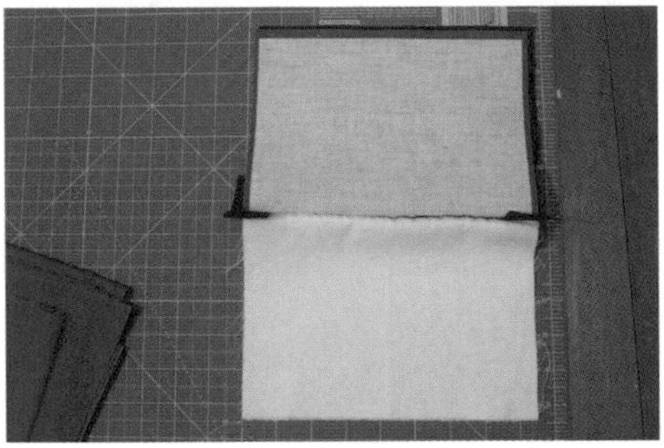

17. Mark the center 3 inches on the bottom of the lining pieces. With a ½-inch seam allowance, stitch from the first mark on the bottom of the lining pieces, around the main pieces, and down to the second mark on the lining pieces. Be careful when you are working near the zipper, so that you don't hit the zipper teeth or stops with your needle.

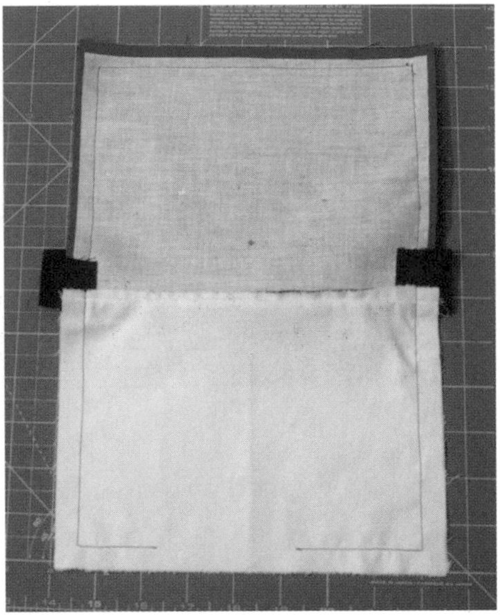

18. Press the bottom seam of the lining open, even across the unsewn part. This will make your final stitching easier.

19. On the main pieces, bring the seam allowances of the corners together and mark a line ⅝ inch away from the ends. Use a pin to make sure the seam allowances are lined up. Stitch across your marks.

20. Reach through the unsewn portion of the lining and turn the entire bag right-side out.

21. Stitch lining closed, either by hand or machine.

Yellow Rose Pin

by Lara Neel

Experience Level: Beginner

Yellow ribbons have had more than one meaning in the United States. At times, they have signified devotion to a loved one or a wish for soldiers to return safely from war. In 1867, Elizabeth Cady Stanton and Susan B. Anthony's suffrage campaign in Kansas used the colors gold and yellow, as well as sunflowers, as symbols of their cause. Nine years later, this song by Marie Le Baron[3] tied yellow ribbons to the suffrage fight.

Oh, we wear a yellow ribbon upon our woman's breast,
We are prouder of its sunny hue than of a royal crest;
'Twas God's own primal color, born of purity and light,
We wear it now for Liberty, for Justice and for Right.
'Tis just a hundred years ago our mothers and our sires,
Lit up, for all the world to see, the flame of freedom's fires;
Through bloodshed and through hardship they labored in the fight;
Today we women labor still for Liberty and Right.
We boast our land of freedom, the unshackling of the slaves;
We point with proud, through bleeding hearts, to myriads of graves.
They tell the story of a war than ended Slavery's night;
And still we women struggle for our Liberty, our Right.

This simple pin is a way to broadcast your support for women's rights. The rose could also be attached to a hair clip back.

3 Le Baron, Marie, "The Yellow Ribbon" song lyrics, ProtestSongLyrics.net. http://www.protestsonglyrics.net/Women_Feminism_Songs/Yellow-Ribbon.phtml

MATERIALS

1½-inch-wide yellow ribbon (see Tips)

Notions

Matching all-purpose thread

Hand-sewing needle

Sew-on pin back

Basic sewing kit

FINISHED MEASUREMENTS

About 2" across

SKILLS NEEDED

You should be comfortable using a sewing machine and working a small amount of hand sewing.

TIPS

- If you have trouble getting the ribbon to gather, lower the top tension on the sewing machine.
- Your ribbon can be of any material, from polyester to silk. Avoid ribbons that have wires in them to make them stiff, as they won't gather well.

CUTTING INSTRUCTIONS

Cut a piece of ribbon that is 24 inches long.

INSTRUCTIONS

1. Leave a long tail of thread hanging from your machine before you start sewing. Do not backstitch at the beginning and end of your work. Using the longest stitch length available, stitch down one long side of your ribbon.

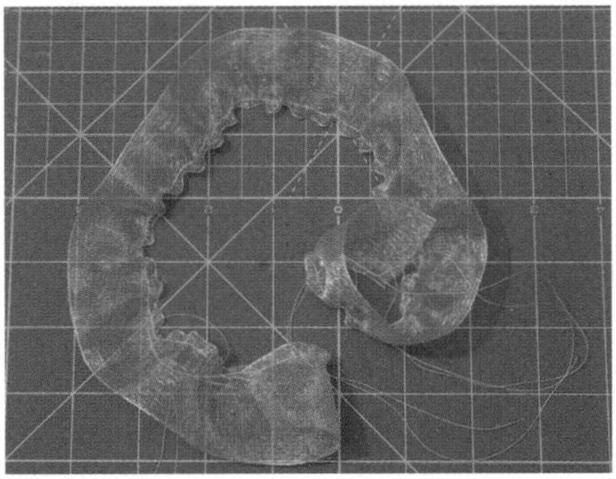

2. Pull on the bobbin thread and gather the edge of the ribbon as tightly as possible.
3. Tie the bobbin and needle threads together on both ends of the ribbon.
4. Thread a hand-sewing needle with one set of the bobbin and needle threads. With a running stitch, stitch along the short edge of the ribbon, then bring the needle back to where it started. Pull tightly to gather the short edge in.

5. Using that gathered short edge as your starting point, roll the ribbon up, holding onto the gathered long edge. Every half turn or so, take a stitch to hold it all together.

6. When you reach the other short end, gather it the same way that you gathered the first short end, and tuck it underneath the rose.

7. Hand stitch the finished rose to the pin back.

Free-Range Pussyhat Symbols

by Lara Neel

Experience Level: Beginner

> Ofglen tells Offred: "I thought you were a true believer . . .
> You were always so stinking pious . . ."
>
> —*The Handmaid's Tale* by Margaret Atwood

I read The Handmaid's Tale *when I was in high school. Among the many lessons it taught me was the importance of broadcasting your beliefs and identity. Without that, people will simply assume you agree with the prevailing order of things.*

The Pussyhat has the ability to mark us out, to one another and to our opponents. But, you simply can't wear a warm hat year-round. I can't, at least. So, I came up with these little symbols, made from felt, that are free-range in that they can go anywhere. I've attached mine to a pin, but you could also support it on a hair clip. This project does not require a sewing machine.

MATERIALS

Scrap of bright pink felt

Scrap of fusible bonding web

Notions

Fabric-marking tool

Small scissors or shears

Matching all-purpose thread

Hand-sewing needle

Sew-on pin back

Iron

Disposable press cloth (see Tips)

Patternmaking supplies or photocopier

FINISHED MEASUREMENTS

About 2" x 1.5" (width x height)

SKILLS NEEDED

You should be comfortable using an iron and working a small amount of hand sewing.

TIPS

- The easiest way to cut out such a small piece, for me, is to trace around the template with a water-soluble marker, then simply cut out the piece with small scissors.

- Felt doesn't have a grain, so you can fit your template pieces in whatever direction works best for you.
- Wool felt is luxurious to work with, but a blended felt or synthetic felt will work, too. If you use a synthetic felt, test to make sure it can survive the amount of heat and steam needed to bond your fusible bonding web.
- Fusible bonding web is awesome, but you should take care not to let it stick to unintended places, like your iron or ironing board. I use tissue paper (the kind you normally use to fill out a gift bag) to protect everything when using most fusibles. In this case, I made a little sandwich. Tissue paper on bottom, followed by the first layer of felt, the fusible bonding web, the second layer of felt and one more layer of tissue paper.

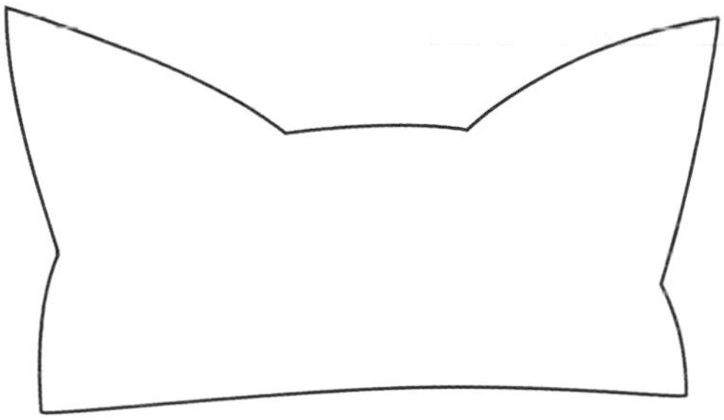

Pg 165: Pussyhat symbol

CUTTING INSTRUCTIONS

Cut 2 pieces of felt, using the pussyhat template on page 165 (see Tips).

Cut 1 piece of fusible bonding web, using the same template.

INSTRUCTIONS

1. Trim away a tiny bit around each edge of the bonding web, to make extra sure that it doesn't extend past the edge of your felt.

2. Following the instructions that came with your bonding web, fuse the two layers of felt to each other.
3. Hand sew your piece to the pin back. Try to pierce only the back layer of felt as you stitch.

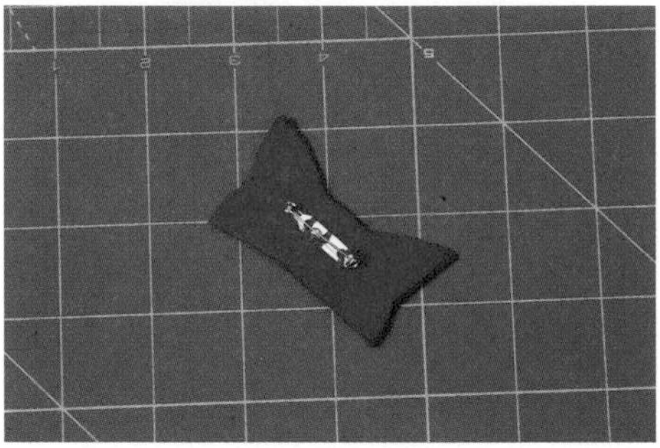

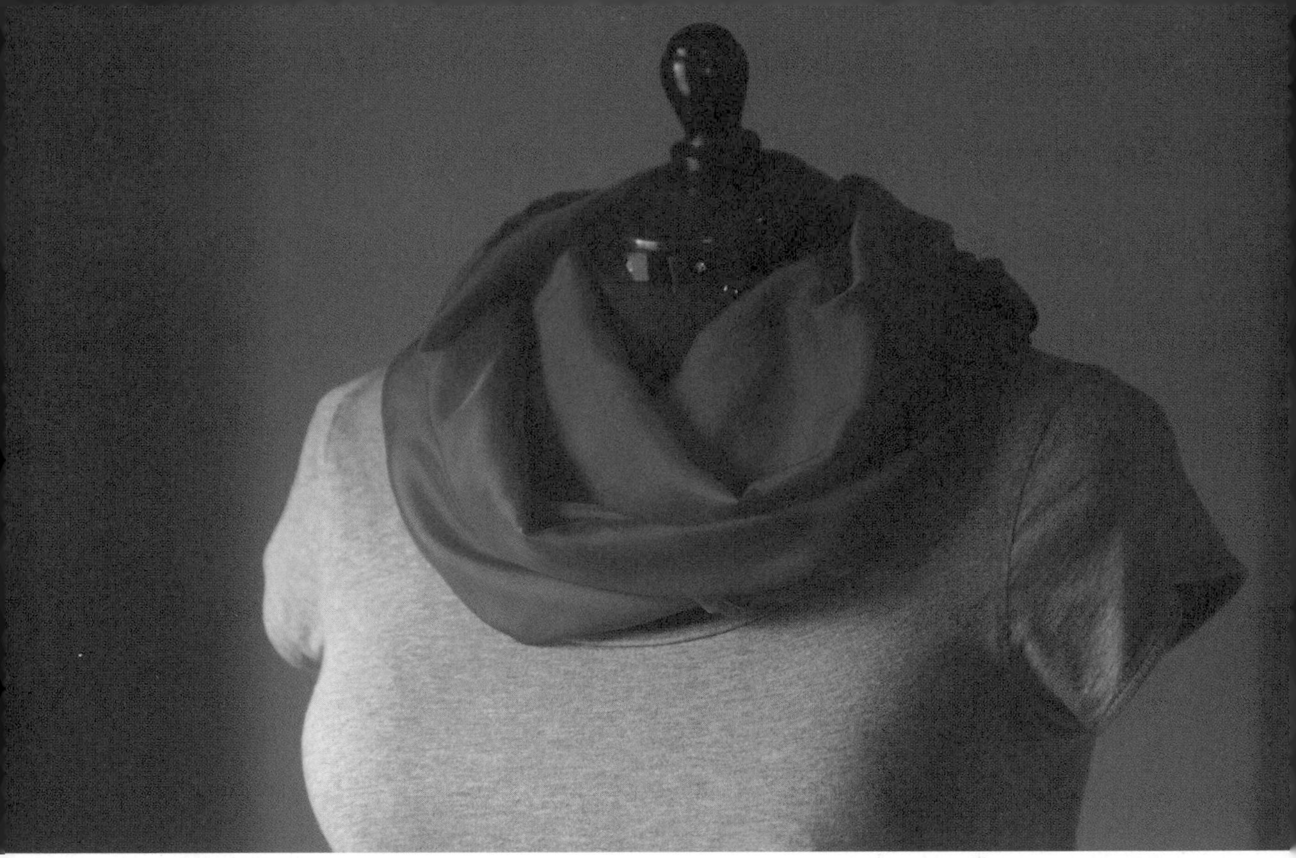

Purple Reins of Power Scarf

by Lara Neel

Experience Level: Advanced Beginner, because of the materials used

No one who lives in Minnesota can escape the hypnotic pull of Prince. My feelings about this singular artist after his 2016 death were captured by K. T. Billey in a piece on *Salon*, "Prince and the Queer Body."[4]

No matter how you feel about The Purple One, a purple scarf is a fairly neutral accessory. Fly it as a flag for the Suffragette movement or just enjoy the pop of color it can add to your day.

Chiffon can be a bit finicky to sew, but this scarf will give you a chance to try it out and practice French seams and narrow hems for tricky fabrics.

MATERIALS

1 yard of chiffon in purple

Notions

Matching all-purpose thread

FINISHED MEASUREMENTS

13.5" x 80" (width x length)

4 Billey, K. T., "Prince and the Queer Body," Salon.com. http://www.salon.com/2016/04/22/prince_and_the_queer_body_our_dirty_patron_saint_of_pop_gave_me_permission_to_think_outside_the_gender_binary/

TIPS

- When you are cutting out your fabric, make sure you leave yourself lots of scraps, so that you can practice stitching and pressing.
- Chiffon can be made of polyester, rayon, or silk. Choose the highest-quality chiffon you can afford. In general, less expensive materials are more difficult to sew.
- Do not backstitch.
- If you find the fabric is being sucked into your throat plate, switch to a straight-stitch presser foot and throat plate.
- Hold the top and bobbin threads when you start your seam.
- You may need to hold your fabric taut as it passes under the needle. Apply gentle, but firm, pressure to the fabric, with one hand in front and one hand in back, to reduce puckering.
- If your seam or hem does pucker, you may feel tempted to press it with a vengeance. This may only make the situation worse by shrinking the thread. Instead, press with the lowest possible setting, and use a press cloth.
- I know sewing instructions often say to use a fresh needle, but this is one time that it really matters. Use an absolutely new sewing needle for this project.

CUTTING INSTRUCTIONS

Make sure your cut edges are perfectly square. Cut two pieces, as long as your fabric is 14½ inches wide. Trim away the selvedge from these pieces. Check them for any imperfections. Trim them both so that they are 4½ inches long.

INSTRUCTIONS

1. Place one piece of your fabric on top of the other, wrong sides together, then stitch along one of the short ends with a -inch seam allowance.
2. Trim this seam allowance to ⅛ inch. Press the seam allowance to one side.

3. Flip the work so that the right sides are together and press the seam again. Stitch along the same short edge again, with a ¼-inch seam allowance, enclosing the raw edges. Press this seam to one side.

4. Lay your work flat. Stitch all around the outside of the scarf with a ¼-inch seam allowance. If your fabric has trouble pivoting at the corners, simply stitch off the edge, cut the threads, and then start the next line of stitching.

5. Press all of the edges to the wrong side along that line of stitching. The stitching gives you something to press against and also reduces the chance of any stretching.

6. While at the machine, fold a hem along the stitching line, then fold again, to enclose the raw edge. Stitch as close to the fold as you can. Complete the hems for the short edges first, then hem the long edges.

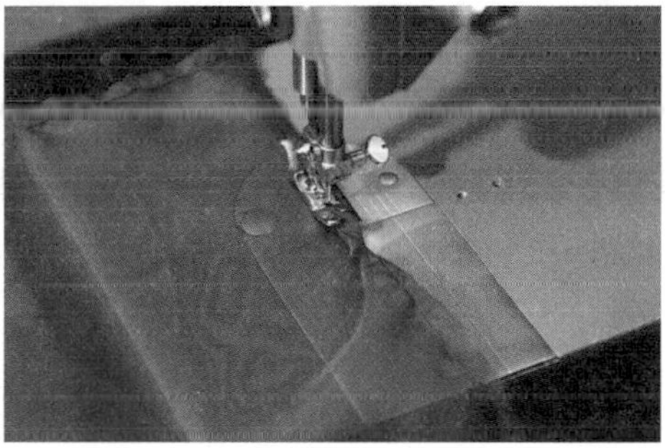

Don't Be Ladylike Cowl

by Heather Marano

Experience Level: Beginner

"Act like a lady." I've always hated that phrase. What does that mean exactly, anyway? Sit still, cross your legs, don't speak unless spoken to. Be demure. Nope, definitely not me. I speak my mind. I'm sometimes crass. I sit cross legged in chairs and on the floor. So this design came to me as a statement piece. It's lofty, light, and that very girly pink, but the addition of the black bows adds a bit of defiance, in my mind. I wear this one doubled up, but it's nice and long and can be worn in a single drape, too. Remind yourself not to be ladylike all the time. Be yourself!

MATERIALS

Yarn:

Knit Picks Aloft in Blush. 72% Super Kid Mohair, 28% Silk; 260 yards/25 g, 2 balls

2 yards of any black yarn of choice to tie bows

Knitting needles: US size 17 (12 mm) circular needles, 32 inches long

Notions

Tapestry needle

Stitch marker

GAUGE

8 stitches and 12 rows over 4 inches

FINISHED MEASUREMENTS

9" x 31"

SKILLS NEEDED

Knitting in the round

TIPS

For knitting abbreviations, see page 175.

INSTRUCTIONS

1. Holding two strands of yarn together (work from both balls at the same time), CO 124 stitches using the long tail cast on.
2. Place a stitch marker and join to work in the round.
3. Knit every round until the piece measures 9 inches from CO edge.
4. Bind off loosely. Weave in the ends.
5. Gather sections of five stitches across a row and tie a bow with the black yarn. Stagger as many of these bows around the cowl as you like. The cowl can be worn long and loose or doubled up.

ABBREVIATIONS

CC: contrasting color

CO: cast on

CH: chain

DC: double crochet

DPN: Double-pointed needle(s)

HDC: half double crochet

K: knit

K2TOG: knit two together

KFB: knit through the front and back loop

M1L: make one left

M1R: make one right

MC: main color

P: purl

PM: place marker

RS: right side

SM: slip marker

SSK: slip, slip, knit

TR: treble crochet

WS: wrong side

WYIB: with yarn in back

WYIF: with yarn in front

CONTRIBUTORS

LARA NEEL

Lara Neel is the author of *Sock Architecture*, a book to inspire the most awesome socks you've ever knit (or just make one of the seventeen patterns in the book). Learn more about her at math4knitters.blogspot.com, where she still blogs about sewing, knitting, and life in general. She published her Step Up Socks patterns because she believes that, no matter how you feel about politics right now, we should all be on our feet, stepping up to the challenges laid before us. She cares about freedom, democracy, women's rights, indigenous rights, and LBGTQIA equality. She's been called a nag more than once, but it bothers her less and less every time.

HEATHER MARANO

Heather Marano has a BA and an MA in Applied Anthropology from the University of South Florida at Tampa. She has studied textiles, fiber processing, spinning, weaving, and knitting among western and non-western cultures. She weaves this knowledge with her work in fiber processing, natural dyeing, spinning, knitting, and knit design. Heather teaches classes on knitting, spinning, and the use of natural dyes. You can follow her on her website themerryspinster.com and on Facebook, Twitter, and Instagram as The Merry Spinster. Her patterns and articles have been published in *Crochet Addict UK*, *Wild Sister Magazine*, *Olann*, and the books *Naming the Goddess* and *The Eternal Thread*. Heather's patterns are available in her Ravelry shop under Heather Marano.

DONNA DRUCHUNAS

Donna Druchunas is obsessed with her family history and the history of knitting. In addition to writing a column, "Our Knitting Roots," she is also running a book club for knitters who want learn to appreciate the people, places, and cultures behind the stitches of their knitting projects. She is the author of many knitting books including her newest titles: *How to Knit Socks that Fit* and *Lithuanian Knitting: Continuing Traditions*. Donna has taught knitting workshops in the United States, Canada, and Europe, and she has five knitting classes on Craftsy. Her newest project is opening a small local yarn shop in rural Vermont where she lives with her husband, mother, three cats, and a long-haired chihuahua. Visit Donna's website at sheeptoshawl.com.

HEIDI HARRIS

Heidi Harris is a native Californian with a Bachelor's Degree in Business Management. She works as a law office manager while also donating time on behalf of nonprofits that are closely aligned with her passions. Shortly after attending her first Fibershed Symposium she discovered her passion for felting. Heidi spearheaded the Fibershed Yurt project, which culminated in displaying locally grown and made fiber art, clothing, and products in a signature yurt entirely hand felted with local wool by Fibershed volunteers. Her latest project is a fiber arts school in Sebastopol, California, that launched in February 2016, in collaboration with Dustin Kahn. Her vision is to create a learning environment that supports the finest teachers in their respective crafts and provides a conducive space for each student to open herself/himself to learning and the creative process.

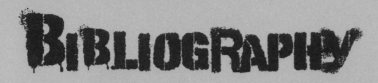

BIBLIOGRAPHY

Adams, Douglas. *The Hitchhiker's Guide to the Galaxy*. New York: Harmony Books, 1979.

Atwood, Margaret. *The Handmaid's Tale*. Boston: Houghton Mifflin, 1986.

Barber, Elizabeth Wayland. *Women's Work: The First 20,000 Years*. New York: Norton, 1994.

Bridenthal, Renate; Koonz, Claudia; and Stuard, Susan. *Becoming Visible: Women in European History*. Houghton Mifflin Company, 1987.

Boston Women's Health Book Collective (ed.). *Our Bodies, Ourselves*. New York: Simon and Schuster, 1976.

Cantarella, Eva. *Pandora's Daughters: The Role and Status of Women in Greek and Roman Antiquity*. The Johns Hopkins University Press, 1987.

DiMassa, Diane. *Complete Hothead Paisan: Homicidal Lesbian Terrorist*. Jersey City: Cleis Press, 1999.

Gies, Frances and Joseph. *Women in the Middle Ages*. Harper and Row, 1978.

Ginsburg, Ruth Bader. *My Own Words*. New York: Simon & Schuster, 2016.

Goldman, Emma. *Anarchism and Other Essays*. Dover Publications, 1969.

Betsy Greer, *Craftivism: The Art and Craft of Activism*. Arsenal Pulp Press, 2014.

Hanauer, Cathi (ed.). *The Bitch in the House*. New York: William Morrow, 2002.

Harper, Kathleen Ann. *The Well-Crafted Mom*. Difference Press, 2015.

hooks, bell. *Art on My Mind: Visual Politics*. New York: New Press, 1995.

hooks, bell. *Feminist Theory: From Margin to Center*. South End Press, 1984.

hooks, bell. *Writing Beyond Race: Living Theory and Practice*. New York, Routledge, 2013.

Ketteler, Judi. *Sew Retro: A Stylish History of The Sewing Revolution*. Voyageur Press, 2010.

Le Guin, Ursula K. *Dancing at the Edge of the World: Thoughts on Words, Women, Places*. Harper and Row, 1989.

Lerner, Gerda. *The Creation of Patriarchy*. Oxford University Press, 1986.

Macdonald, Anne L. *No Idle Hands: The Social History of American Knitting*. New York: Ballantine Books, 1988.

O'Faolain, Julia, and Martines, Lauro. *Not in God's Image: Women in History from the Greeks to the Victorians.* Harper and Row, 1973.

Orwell, George. *Nineteen Eighty-Four.* London: Secker & Warburg, 1949.

Plant, Judith. *Healing the Wounds: The Promise of Ecofeminism.* New Society Publishers, 1989.

Rigdon, Renee and Stewart, Zabet. *Anticraft: Knitting Beading and Stitching for the Slightly Sinister.* Cincinnati: North Light Books, 2007.

SARK. *Succulent Wild Woman: Dancing with Your Wonder-full Self!* Simon and Schuster, 1997.

Steinem, Gloria. *My Life on the Road.* New York: Random House, 2015.

Walker, Barbara G. *The Skeptical Feminist: Discovering the Virgin, Mother, and Crone.* San Francisco: Harper & Row, 1987.

Walker, Barbara G. *The Woman's Dictionary of Symbols and Sacred Objects.* San Francisco, CA: Harper & Row, 1988.

West, Lindy. *Shrill.* New York: Hachette Books, 2016.

Some of Our Favorite Organizations and Resources

American Civil Liberties Union

www.aclu.org

Bitch Media

www.bitchmedia.org

Fibershed

www.fibershed.com

Human Rights Campaign

www.hrc.org

Modeknit Yarn

modeknit.com

Ms. Magazine

www.msmagazine.com

Planned Parenthood

www.plannedparenthood.org

Southern Poverty Law Center

www.splcenter.org

Stories in Stitches

storiesinstitches.net

West County Fiber Arts

westcountyfiberarts.com